EDVARD MUNCH

PHAIDON

THE WANDERER BY NIGHT. SELF-PORTRAIT. 1939.

EDVARD MUNCH

BY OTTO BENESCH

WITH EIGHTY-NINE ILLUSTRATIONS
INCLUDING TWENTY-THREE
IN FULL COLOUR

PHAIDON PUBLISHERS INC
DISTRIBUTED BY DOUBLEDAY AND COMPANY INC
GARDEN CITY · NEW YORK

TRANSLATED FROM THE GERMAN
BY JOAN SPENCER

© PHAIDON PRESS LTD · LONDON
5 CROMWELL PLACE · SW7
MADE IN GREAT BRITAIN 1960
PRINTED BY HUNT · BARNARD & CO LTD · AYLESBURY · BUCKS

EDVARD MUNCH

PRELUDE

EUROPEAN ART at the turn of the last century was striving for 'style'. What does this mean? Let us attempt a brief answer to this question by giving a few definitions of this concept. Naturalistic detail gives place to typical form; the transitory gives place to the permanent and eternally valid; the fleeting, chance impression gives place to the monumental, stable, architectonic and decorative; the rendering of a visual impression of reality gives place to an art which enhances or transcends reality and endeavours to give visible form to general human values, eternal forces of life and the world of ideas. Around 1900 'style' meant an art that does not copy nature but enhances it or turns aside from it if the language of expression in line, form and colour so demands. The fulfilment of this tendency was seen in a new kind of monumental painting.

The three most important painters of this general European movement were Ferdinand Hodler, Gustav Klimt, and Edvard Munch. These painters regarded monumental tasks as the very goal of their creative activity. That this aim could be realized only fragmentarily is explained by the problems of the age in which they lived and by the position of the artist in society. The greatest of them was Munch. Klimt's career came to an early end and the fruits of his achievement were reaped by the young Expressionists Schiele and Kokoschka; Hodler did not always avoid the danger of a grandiose formal rigidity which prevented his assuming the role of guide and mentor to younger generations; it was Munch who until his death at the age of eighty discharged this function in his art which, for all its homogeneity, is eternally alive, fluid and constantly renewed. Munch became Expressionism's man of destiny. The works fulfilling this mission began to take shape as early as the 1890's. We must therefore look back in history if we wish to understand the towering figure of this artist and the vital part he played in contemporary art until the day of his death.

Edvard Munch was born on December 12, 1863 at Løiten in the province of Hedemarken in Norway. A Norwegian, he belonged to a nation which played no part in modern art until the nineteenth century. As in Russia, the nineteenth century saw in Scandinavia the triumphant emergence of a new literature, in which it fell to Norway to play a leading role. This brought in its train an artistic revolution too. Inspired by French Impressionism, a group of *avant-garde* painters was formed who were intellectually in sympathy with the new writers. This was the world into which Munch was born. He was a physician's son with a brother and three sisters. His family came of a long line of priests, scholars and officials, whose social status had declined from the intellectual patriciate to the petite bourgeoisie. Its mental attitude was devout and other-worldly. The bent towards mysticism is peculiar to many Scandinavians. Mysticism formed the background of Nordic religious thought from Saint Birgitta to Swedenborg, and in the nineteenth century it invaded also pictorial art. Munch marks its appearance in modern painting, just as did Ibsen and Strindberg in modern literature. In her last will Munch's mother wrote the following words for her son: 'Strive for the things above, and not for things on earth.' This religious, ascetic view of life, rooted in pietism, ran through the entire family. Munch's letters attest the strength of his family ties. The death of his mother and still more the death of a sister dealt the young man a shattering blow which left enduring traces in his creative work. The austere, imposing figure of his sister Inger appears in the most splendid of his early portraits. Munch never married. Most of his letters were written to Inger, and to his foster-mother whose portrait, painted in 1884 (Plate 2), is one of his most beautiful impressionistic studies. His family provided him with his earliest models and gave him the first stimulus to larger compositions.

The light of the spiritual and intellectual world which Munch's art endeavours to make manifest is encompassed with daemonic darkness, which appears now as the active power of sin, now as melancholy, the darkness of the soul. It is a dualistic world. It will become clear from the analysis of his works how great was the role of the daemonic element in his art. He captured and held it in his art and led the powers of light to victory. But without the darkness the light would be less convincing. The 'second sight' of the Nordic people became for him an artistic intuition. Hence the basic character of Munch's work was always felt by his contemporaries to be visionary, despite the power and directness of his approach to the world of the senses.

Munch's milieu and place of birth meant that he grew up in a narrow provincialism. The wider European artistic movements or works of art reached him only at second-hand. The originality of Munch's genius stands out with surprising clarity in his very earliest work (Plate 1).

The artistic language of the future which he fashioned was not the result of outside stimulus but was a mode of expression developed from within and absolutely his own. When he did receive his first decisive impressions in France he met them already half-way. He had no real tuition but ought rather to be termed self-taught. Work in the company of like-minded friends developed to early mastery his irresistible artistic urge, which his family accepted with very bad grace. At first he attended the art school run by the sculptor Julius Middelthun. Later he joined a group of young painters who worked in the same building as did the pioneers of Norwegian Impressionism: Christian Krohg, Erik Theodor Werenskiold and Hans Olaf Heyerdahl. Munch felt particularly indebted to the latter. These artists were the revolutionaries of the eighties who discovered Norway and portrayed realistically her landscape and her people: they were in fact Realists of an Impressionistic brand. They admired Manet and had formed their style on the French School. The enthusiastic support these Realist painters afforded the young man cannot be valued too highly. Krohg, Werenskiold and the landscape painter Frits Thaulow were the first enthusiastic defenders of Munch's early works in word, deed, or writing. A breath of fresh air invaded the stuffy provincial atmosphere. The older painters inspired the younger ones with the idea of a European style of painting. Paris was the artists' Mecca. Munch spent a few weeks there in 1885, but did not then come into contact with contemporary French art, though Rembrandt and the examples of the Spanish School in the Louvre made a deep impression on him. In the early- and mid-eighties he painted mostly portraits and landscape studies. They show Munch embarked on a chiaroscuro style which falls within the broader scope of Courbet's European influence, the kind of chiaroscuro that was exemplified at that time in Munich by Leibl and his circle. But Munch did not stop short at the mastery in his art of the purely pictorial aspect of reality: he went further. There is among his early masterpieces a striking portrait of his sister Inger, painted in 1884 (Plate 4). The shy embarrassment of the girl's proud figure, her face and hands luminous in the darkness, remotely anticipate the work of the young Egon Schiele. Munch's closest artist friends were the supremely talented Kalle Løchen and the landscape painter Jørgen Sørensen, who modelled his work on Pissarro and Sisley. The portrait of Sørensen (Thiis p. 113) that Munch painted in 1885 shows the head bright against a dark background, glowing with an inner light, seeming to radiate an aura of its own; and the comparison with Oskar Kokoschka's early work is inescapable. Thus in his 'Naturalist' pictures Munch already sounds his own characteristic note which heralds Expressionism and the visionary element. We encounter the same phenomenon in James Ensor's impressionistic pictures of the early 'eighties.

The autumn exhibitions in Kristiania (named Oslo since 1924) like the Salon d'automne in Paris, always mustered the *avant-garde*. Here

5

Munch exhibited his earliest work. From the world of Naturalism and Impressionism emerged the decisive achievement of this twenty-three year-old: *The Sick Child* (Plate 3). Munch worked at the painting a long time – from 1885 to 86. Layer after layer of colour was scraped off, obliterated, and tried afresh time and again. Public indignation was aroused against the young painter for daring to exhibit as completed work what was regarded as an 'unfinished attempt'. The very length and intensity of his labours prove that it is anything but an unfinished attempt. To break through the naturalistic mode of vision meant a painful struggle. The three-dimensional illusion is discarded. The sick child, the mother with her head bent in sorrow, and the table with the glass on it, fit into a geometrical arrangement of blocks and flat surfaces, without any illusion of perspective, which is far removed from the chance effects of Impressionism. This looser style of painting does in fact remind one of Impressionism, but the scratching and scraping of the surface produced a novel pictorial structure quite foreign to Impressionism. A curious parallel suggests itself with the contemporary works of Seurat, though Munch lacked his methodical organization and certainly did not know Seurat at this time. The colours are cool tones of blue-green, grey-blue, and olive-grey, in the middle of which the fiery red of the hair is ablaze on a white pillow. Even this colour has an unreal, visionary quality. The objects (the tumbler, the curtain) tremble and quiver in a fluid that seems to fill the room, like a metaphysical essence. This was an entirely new language of forms which corresponded to the touching nature of the subject. The painter himself confessed: 'Most of my later work had its origin in this picture.' There are echoes in this painting of the shock the artist sustained in the death of one of his sisters. The deliberate destruction of the compact areas of pigment makes the solid form appear transparent and reveals behind it something which could not have been shown if the coloured surface only had been faithfully rendered. The picture takes as its subject people who by their suffering or by their compassion, experience the transition from this world to the world beyond. It is the beginning of the long series of Munch's sick-room and death-bed scenes. The composition – an arrangement of lasting validity – was repeated by Munch four times in dated paintings (1896, 1906, 1907, 1926), with hardly any alteration except for the pictorial structure. We shall return later to this phenomenon of the constant recurrence of certain pictorial ideas in Munch's work.

This early masterpiece furthered the emergence of Munch's individual, highly personal style which did at the same time realize in the highest degree the artistic aims of his time. His artist friends sensed that something new was in the making. Munch presented the picture to his friend Krohg, who was enthusiastic in its defence. Krohg was not yet able to define accurately the new departure implied by this picture; he saw in it the fulfilment of Impressionism. That is why he wrote in 1886: 'We, the generation of painters to which I belong, are not, unfortunately, Impressionists. We may only stand on the mountain-top and look down into the Promised Land. . . . *He* is an Impressionist, our only one hitherto.' And yet Munch had, in this work, gone far beyond Impressionism.

Munch received considerable moral support from his older friends and those of his own age. This was the decade of the *Kristiania-Bohème* (Oslo, Kommunes Kunstsamlinger), portrayed by Munch's friend the Hegelian and radical social philosopher Hans Jaeger (Plate 5) in a famous, not to say notorious book which earned its author a prison sentence and split the entire Norwegian intelligentsia into two camps. The social radicalism of literature and poetry went hand in hand with the realism of the pictorial arts. Also Ibsen was regarded as a 'Realist' by his contemporaries, whereas Munch, on whom he made a deep impression, already perceived in Ibsen's works the resonance of those other ideas so close to his own aspirations. The new literature and painting were felt to be social in implication, and gave rise to stormy debates in the studios and cafés. The cruel spiritual problems of the first version (since destroyed) of Munch's paintings *The Day After* (Plate 25) and *Puberty* (Plate 12) passed unrecognized. Society and the prevailing mental attitude were such as described by Strindberg in his novel *The Red Room*.

Although this milieu may have contributed to Munch's intellectual formation, spiritually he rose above it. The historic contact with Krohg's and Heyerdahl's Naturalism may be traced in those landscapes into which Munch introduced his sisters Laura (Plate 6) and Inger as 'staffage'. The interaction of man and landscape is specific to Munch's work – each is a function of the other. For Manet and his Norwegian imitators this was essentially a visual and pictorial problem, but for Munch a problem of content. The thoughtful, contemplative, melancholy absorption of his figures bears witness to questions of ultimate and paramount importance. It finds an echo in the curiously withdrawn landscape, serious even in broad daylight. The picture painted in 1889, *Evening Hour* (Plate 9), combines the portraits of Inger and the poet Bødtker. The inner being of these two grave, silent figures, the content of their wordless dialogue, dies away in the landscape. These are the reserved, taciturn people we meet in Hamsun's beautiful early works: *Hunger*, *Mysteries* and *Pan*, which was one of

7

Munch's favourite books. How much 'style' is already evident in such a naturalistic picture! Both figures are conceived as tall columns. The steep curve of the hat the man is wearing reminds one how, in Cézanne's and Marées' portraits such headgear seems part of the wearer. This curve is repeated below in the tight fit of the jacket. A similar economy and constriction of curve is seen in the figure of the woman. They indicate a hermetic self-absorption. The conical forms of the figures, which in subsequent pictures tend to resemble simple pillars of salt, recur in the bushes and vegetation in the landscape. This picture, too, has captured a fragment of the infinite, as did the Impressionists, but how much more carefully constructed this picture is, and how it vibrates with inner emotion! How daringly does the painter cut the picture in two with the vertical line of the woman and the hedge behind her! The hedge springs up into the limitless space, and the figures, cut below, stretch down into the bottomless depth. Similar compositional elements are found in *The Sick Child*. The colour range differs considerably from that of the Impressionists. It is built up of cool tones of blue, lilac, and green, with a little ochreish-brown. There, too, the tendency to stylization prevails. Munch's 'période bleue' came a decade before Picasso's.

The same year saw the completion of a new large version of the theme the *Sick Child* in horizontal format with the title *Spring* (Plate 8). The child, looked after by her mother, is sitting in a room flooded with spring sunshine; the curtains billow out in the light breeze, thus introducing curves into the picture. 1889 brought a decisive turn of fortune. Munch arranged his first one-man show at the Progressive Students' Union. This exhibition, and the powerful aid of his old friends in the Realist camp who, like Werenskiold, had by now attained to academic dignities, gained him a state bursary to run for several years. Eager to learn, he entered the workshop of the renowned teacher Léon Bonnat, but the young master had already developed far beyond the tuition he could obtain there. After several weeks he left Bonnat's workshop and continued to work on his own account. Of far greater significance for him was the modern French School of painting which could be seen that same year in a magnificent centenary exhibition ranging from David and Delacroix to the Impressionists, on show at the Paris World's Fair. There, too, Eiffel and Dutert erected their first steel constructions, which, according to Munch's own words made a deep impression on him. He stepped out of the narrow provincialism of his homeland into the wide world, thus determining his role as a European artist. From now on Munch was at home only for short spells, usually in the summer. He began living abroad, and until 1892 he lived mainly in France.

8

At first French Impressionism made a powerful impact on Munch. He painted a picture of the main street of his home town, *Karl-Johan Street* (Glaser Fig. 9), a long, melancholy, cold, Scandinavian boulevard in the autumn rain. This painting, executed in 1889, shows him as a faithful follower of Pissarro. Another view of the same street in the sunshine, with a military band advancing along it, shows Munch as a follower of Manet (Plate 7).

Early in 1890 Munch withdrew to St. Cloud to stay with his friend Goldstein, the Danish poet. There he painted a picture of decisive importance: *Night* (Plate 11). It portrays a silent, moonlit interior. Individual objects are engulfed in obscurity or semi-obscurity. His friend, wearing a top-hat, sits wraith-like by the window looking out at the Seine, where a steamer glides past the square of the window frame. The moon paints a pale rectangle on the floor, impressively crossed by the window bars. A fold of curtain fills the lower left-hand corner as a foil; a shadowy lantern swings at the window. That is all the picture contains – and yet how rich it is, how dense, how laden with significant form! Never before were silent, shadowy, disembodied objects rendered so eloquent. They speak the language Rilke tells of in his *Aufzeichnungen des Malte Laurids Brigge*. Matter recedes, leaving only its impact behind, for here may be found the heart of things. This is what Munch said of the task of modern art: 'For Realism it was the façade that counted, for Impressionism the character. Now it is shadows and movements. . . . Such shadows as the prisoner sees in his cell, those curious grey streaks of shadow which flee and then return, which slide apart and come together again like fans, bending, curving, dividing.' One need hardly stress the fact that here Munch has not merely solved a visual, formal problem, but that the picture is also full of mystery, full of muted tragedy and lyrical expectancy.

Two questions force themselves upon us. What did Munch see in Paris? Which modern paintings impressed him? The answer comes from the works themselves. For this picture the answer is: Seurat. In Seurat he saw a firm, taut, simple yet refined pictorial composition in which matter is transformed into vibrations of colour. The difference between Seurat and Munch is that Munch was not interested in the scientific analysis of light into the colours of the spectrum. He called his picture *Symphony in Blue*. Also there is greater poetic content in Munch than in Seurat. This is true of the 1891 night pieces painted in the same style as the landscape of Nice, the portrait of Mrs. Thaulow and the first version of the *Kiss*, in which two lovers stand before a window and embrace in the darkness.

In 1891 Munch also painted two Paris street scenes: *Rue Lafayette*

9

(Plate 10) and *Rue de Rivoli*, seen from the top storey, vibrating and shimmering in the sunshine. They remind one of works by the Neo-Impressionists Signac and H.-E. Cross, but far surpass them in the expression of the elementary movement of light. A view of *Karl-Johan Street* (Thiis p. 179) drenched in sunlight, painted the same year, also shows Munch's transition from the Impressionist into the Neo-Impressionist mode of vision.

It must not be supposed that Munch's contact with contemporary French painting meant a sudden overwhelming rush of impressions. His spiritual development was already too firmly advanced for that. He merely accepted whatever suited his own endeavour. His stay in France was not the only source of impressions important for his art; they continued in Berlin where dealers and collectors interested themselves in modern French art. In later years Munch returned to Paris several times. His relation to French art must be constantly re-examined in the light of the works produced at the time. However, during his first prolonged stay in France, Munch must certainly have become acquainted with the works of the three great Post-Impressionists Seurat, Van Gogh, and Gauguin. Perhaps he also became acquainted with the works of the 'Nabis' and Toulouse-Lautrec, which were particularly significant for him in his second Paris period (1896–7), and which acquired a special importance for his graphic art.

THE WORLD OF POETRY

THE REALLY IMPORTANT turning-point in Munch's creative activity which set the final stamp on his style during the nineties, occurred in 1892. It resulted in the monumental full-length portrait of his sister Inger (Plate 13), wearing a dark dress with light pattern. It is one of the most important works in European painting at the close of the century. The last vestige of tonality following the model of the old masters, which still dominated the first portrait of Inger in 1884, has disappeared. So has the impressionistic dissolution into light and atmosphere which characterizes the works of 1888. The firm outline appears completely to flatten the figure in its black dress with violet pattern. The decorative manner of 'Art Nouveau' comes to the fore. The distribution of flat surfaces and lines is of refined simplicity. At the point where the smooth wall begins, a horizontal line balances the vertical ones. The figure is set slightly to the right of centre, thus producing that asymmetrical effect so highly important to the newer architecture and decorative arts. Nowadays, of course, one overlooks the decorative effect intended at the time, enthralled by the austerity, the infinite seriousness of this countenance gazing from the canvas like one of the Fates. The brushwork is broad and loose. This loosening is transformed into a new firmness and a clarity both of surfaces as well as of their outlines – yet without any loss of atmospheric quality. The woman diffuses her own delicate essence, an intellectual rather than a visual effect.

Again we are forcibly reminded of Seurat and those calm, statuesque female figures in his *Sunday Afternoon on the Grande Jatte* in which all the shimmering fluidity of the Impressionists is transformed into something three-dimensional and architectural. Inger's portrait is anticipated by the portrait of Mrs. Thaulow, painted the year before. Its pulsating brushwork is reminiscent of that of Seurat's studies. Now all this has disappeared. The only other paintings containing figures of such simplicity, such great dimensions, outlined with such undulating curves, are those of Gauguin and his followers the 'Nabis'. The intensity and concentration of the human element reminds one of Van Gogh's *Arlésienne*.

This picture marks the decisive turning-point from Naturalism and Impressionism to 'Style'. Also Munch's contemporaries felt he had turned to an art-form which expressed purely in terms of paint, the new idealism and its poetic and intellectual content. After his years of work in France he held a one-man show in the Tostrupgården in Oslo; in the catalogue the pictures were entitled according to their colour or light effect: *Harmony in Black and Violet* (the portrait of Inger), *Study in Blue, Evening, Twilight*, with the addition of the adjective 'sombre' to emphasize the lyrical element. One title runs: *The Mystic of a Summer Night*. (Hodin 95).

One work dating from 1891 caused a great stir amongst his artist friends. It appears under various titles: *Melancholia*, *The Yellow Boat* and *Jealousy* (Plate 14). First Munch made a pastel (1891), but in 1895 he repeated it in oil. It is a landscape of Åsgårdstrand, where Munch usually spent the summer. The twilight causes details to blend and fuse into broad patches. Wavy contours link background with foreground, forming a decorative unity of surface. Massive boulders, light-coloured along the shore, turn dark in the shallows, casting reflections. The undulating line of the wood is continued along a spit of land and dies away among the clouds of the evening sky. One solitary house is

11

absorbed by these wavy lines. Along the fine, clear horizontal line of the jetty a man and woman walk towards a waiting boat. From this melancholy, oppressive evening atmosphere a wordless drama emerges. In the lower right-hand corner of the picture appears, in close-up, the head of a man sunk in reverie. His thoughts revolve round the couple approaching the yellow boat. There the landscape comes to life. The boulders on the shore, shaped somewhat like the man's head, converse secretly of the dark thoughts seething in his mind. The stones in the water become dark eyes spying out wanton acts. All along the shore the water drips and trickles like the harbinger of some dreadful tidings. And all this appears as the pure language of form, rather as in works by Henry Moore, without the slightest literary allusion to point it. Krohg wrote of this picture: 'Our thanks are due to Munch for making the boat yellow; but for this the picture would not have been painted. And what of the colours? A magical violet dotted here and there with venomous green patches – most awe-inspiring. Patches in which we can loose ourselves and thus become better men. Serious and austere, almost religious. It is akin to Symbolism, that latest salvation of French art. ... Has anyone heard such resonant colours as there are in this picture? It borders on music rather than painting. ... And thus we have the rare phenomenon that Munch, regarded here at home as the most ruthless Realist of all, as the foremost and boldest of all painters of the ugly, is the first and only painter to turn to Idealism, to dare to make his model, Nature, bow to his mood so as to attain to loftier things.'

But for Gauguin such a transformation would not have been possible. Gauguin, who was Thaulow's brother-in-law and exhibited alongside the Norwegians in Kristiania in 1885, was no stranger to Munch. The year Munch appeared in Paris he was living in Brittany where there formed around him the so-called Pont-Aven School, a colony of painters of kindred aims. Gauguin's first religious pictures were painted at this time. Let us examine the painting entitled *The Yellow Christ* (1889). The Breton landscape is summarized in large synthetic forms. The forest is a dark mass with blobs of colour indicating the tree-tops, and the fields form huge flat expanses devoid of perspective. The faces are indeterminate masks in which eyes, nose, and mouth are indicated by some blurred marks. In the same way the face of the man in Munch's painting *Jealousy* is almost completely extinguished, only the dark brows remaining as the menacing outward sign of his brooding. It was a Breton peasant sculpture that inspired Gauguin to use a similar strict economy of line in his *Christ*. One also finds in Gauguin the same emphasis on the undulating line which has intrinsic, ornamental value as an expressive symbol. Gauguin was an artist who first manifested the stylistic devices of 'Art Nouveau' with a tendency towards the decorative, but instead of remaining decorative his work develops further and becomes the symbolism of a new, enhanced sensibility with spiritual aspirations. His work is eloquent with a longing for the 'Primitive', whereby art would regain its simplicity and conviction. In Gauguin, too, we first encounter those luminous, unbroken, decoratively abstract colours which originate not in the contemplation of nature but in his own inner vision.

The first version of *Jealousy* marks the beginning of those richly significant themes which were soon to suggest the conception of a cyclic presentation of human life. An art in quest of a new form had in finding it, also found a fresh content.

Munch's progress along this path is evidenced by impressions from the *Gambling Hall at Monte Carlo* (Plate 17) painted from memory, and by the second version of the *Kiss* in 1892 (Plate 16) with a view of a street in Nice, a towering cypress in the foreground. One of Munch's most magnificent paintings, usually assigned too early a date, is certainly later than the portrait of Inger. It concludes the variations on the motif treated repeatedly by Munch during his Impressionistic period – the picture *Karl-Johan Street* (1892; Plate 15). We see the street in the evening light, crowded and animated. The painter is walking towards the stream of people. It is growing dark, individual forms merge into great masses, windows gleam ghost-like through the dusk. The passers-by are ghost-like too, under the last pale reflection of the fading light – nameless spectres from an unknown world with pallid death-masks for faces. All individuality, all humanity is drained from these faces, which seem transfixed by some inexplicable event, some elemental fate which unites them all in one identity. The theme treated later by Munch in the composition entitled *Anxiety* is here touched on for the first time.

All these works mark the transition to simplified flat surfaces and synthesis of line – a kind of expressive poster style.

As a result of the exhibition Munch held in Kristiania in 1892, a year most fateful for his development, he received an invitation from the Association of Berlin Painters (arranged by the Norwegian painter Normann) to exhibit his collected works. Immediately after the opening a scandal broke out. By a narrow majority the Association obliged the exhibition to close. The progressive artists, led by Walter Leistikow and including among others Max Liebermann, Karl Köpping, and Ludwig von Hofmann, championed Munch. This split within the Association led to the foundation of the 'New Secession',

13

Berlin's most important and most progressive association of artists. 'The Munch Case' was a European sensation which made the painter famous overnight. Invitations to Cologne and Düsseldorf followed. Munch found himself acclaimed in Germany by a numerous *avant-garde* of German artistic and intellectual life, who prevailed on him to settle in Berlin where he lived from 1892 until 1895. The fact that Munch was a Scandinavian was an advantage – there was great enthusiasm for Scandinavian literature, and hence an interest in Nordic scenery and art. Leistikow, himself an outstanding landscape painter, was an ardent supporter of Munch's, for he recognized in Munch's pictures an aim akin to his own striving for conciseness and 'style'. Let us compare Leistikow's *Danish Castle in a Park* with the landscape of Munch's *Jealousy*. Here, too, the woods are compressed into dark masses, a type of architectural arrangement which breathes a grave, melancholy mood. Here, too, we encounter an elimination of detail and a concentration upon essentials. It is a related striving for 'style'. Just as the new decorative style in Paris developed from Gauguin's desire for style to the stylistic surge of 'Art Nouveau' – represented in France by the architects Baudot and Guimard, in Belgium by Horta and Van de Velde – so there arose in Germany 'Jugendstil', in Austria 'Secession' and 'Ver Sacrum'. Otto Eckmann, Hermann Obrist, and Leistikow himself brought about the success of the new arts and crafts, the new art of interior decoration. So it was that Munch, because of the similarity of his aims, received powerful support from current trends in taste. His stylistic aim was of course conditioned by his search for new values of expression, but this did not prevent a formal coincidence with the products of 'Jugendstil'. A glance at a wallpaper design by Leistikow with wavy motifs of plants and flowers reminiscent of reflections in water reveals that a similar formal structure also appears in a picture from Munch's Berlin period: *The Cry* (1893; Plate 19). But what a tragic anguish of spirit Munch conjures up by means of similar decorative wavy forms! Set in a landscape of Nordic fjords a breathtakingly foreshortened jetty rushes out to meet us. It is a movement in space which portrays a paroxysm of harried flight. As an embodiment of this feeling there leaps out of the picture the figure of a woman, all the remaining force of her being concentrated in the scream issuing from her gaping mouth. She is pursued by something unknown, something nameless that exists only in her own mind, for the blurred figures in the distance, despite their sinister anonymity, are hardly pursuers but rather passive strollers. The daemon dwells in the hunted woman herself, so that she blazes like a flame of horror, while the landscape, set on fire by her, streams away from her like molten lava, to die away

14

in the undulating lines of an evening sky of fiery red and sulphur yellow. The oscillations of matter are no longer optical phenomena but the acoustic figures of that scream. It is only by eliminating all naturalistic statement, by blending foreground with background in one great linear design, that this totality and compelling unity of expression is achieved. It might be said that with this picture Expressionism was born. The idea goes back to 1891 when Munch took up the locality without 'staffage' as a study from nature at Nice. This Nordic scene with a blood-red evening sky was already given shape in a painting dated 1892, except that in the foreground the half-length figure of a man seen in lost profile is staring fixedly at the landscape: it bears the title *Despair*. The catastrophic release of this anguish is then portrayed in the present picture. Munch lithographed it in 1895, and wrote the following words on the print: '*The Cry*. I felt this great cry throughout Nature.' He thus made it clear that the primary experience is nature and scenery, and the terrified figure of a woman merely a symbolic expression of it. Panic in nature, as expressed by Hamsun in his contemporary novels, *Hunger, Mysteries, Pan*, assumed this form.

This art, which strikes us as the essence of personal creativeness, has also its historical roots. In Van Gogh's *Railway Passage* of 1888 (De la Faille 507), we see a similar boldly widening perspective, a similar panic-stricken spatial experience, full of anguish and menacing catastrophe: a pavement becomes a frantically rolling carpet with a dark human figure at the end. This enhanced awareness of space, obtained by sudden effects of perspective, will be found repeatedly in Munch's work in constantly fresh forms. Munch's undulating line, the glowing decorative colours as an expression of a heightened spiritual life, are encountered a hundred years earlier in the water-colours and prints of the English mystic William Blake. I refer to Los in the philosophical composition *The Book of Urizen*. The horror that pervades Los' entire being so that he is consumed with flame, is concentrated here, too, in one tremendous cry. I am convinced that Munch knew some of Blake's work and derived inspiration from them.

The observation of a phenomenon of light again assumes a similar mythical grandeur in *Moonlight* (1893; Plate 21). A length of garden fence and the corner of a Scandinavian wooden house gleam in the soft light of the moon. In front of the fence the tall figure of a woman is dimly perceived – her role is the same as that of Mrs. Thaulow and Inger in earlier pictures. Her pale, ghostly face, set on the dark column of her body, gleams in the moonlight, as does every other object, but it is far more transparent, impalpable, ghostly. The shadow she casts on the wall of the house becomes another living creature watching over her, dark and threatening – whether to protect and defend or to harm and admonish no-one can tell. And the woman's contours, guessed at rather than seen, are repeated in the darker half of the picture where they spring to life in shadowy, undulating lines, visibly linking her with the realm of shadows but also expressing symbolically her subjection to the mighty powers of fate prevailing throughout nature. Similarly, in *Puberty*, the shadow thrown on the wall of the room by the naked girl assumes a life of its own, either watching over her or threatening her.

Munch's contacts in Berlin with literary circles were more important for him than those with artistic ones. German art in the nineties had little to offer anyone fresh from Paris. The spiritual tension of Munch's work had no equal in German painting at that time, but in literature it had. Nothing is known of a meeting between Munch and Stefan George, who was a friend of one of Munch's ardent supporters, Ludwig von Hofmann. The artists of George's circle were epigones clinging to a decorative style, capable only of embellishing with superficial ornament the glowing world of the poet and falling far short of his eminence. But there was in Germany at that time *one* painter who equalled him in stature: Munch. There is a painting by Munch – one of his finest – which is a monument equal to the lofty grandeur of George's spirit, expressed at that time in the sonorous lines of his *Hymnen, Pilgerfahrten,* and *Algabal,* namely, *The Storm* (Plate 23) painted in 1893. It portrays an anonymous nocturnal landscape showing the outskirts of a town with scattered houses standing in walled gardens, perhaps on the sea-shore, judging by the phosphorescent wavy lines and the gigantic boulders and flat rocks gleaming eerily through the darkness. It is a no man's land faintly illumined by the pale lightning. The storm blusters through the picture, not bent on destroying the face of a peaceful world but called into being by this ghostly world itself, seemingly born of the trees, the house-fronts, all these mysterious lines, forms, surfaces, dots. The whole picture shudders before the fiery breath of this raging storm. It is a lofty and terrible world now becoming the scene of a solemn event. As if on the stage of a classical tragedy the light figure of a girl detaches itself from the gloom, and advances as a protagonist towards the danger zone at the picture's edge where, erect and unapproachable as a flame, she faces destruction. The chorus of lamentation behind her merges into a confused anxious mass with arms upraised and faces hidden in their hands from terror, divined rather than perceived. What we encounter here is a poetic event in which horror is turned to beauty, as miraculous as the enchanting, phosphorescent, opalescent colours, glowing mysteriously throughout the picture.

16

Fig. 1. CHAMBER OF DEATH. Lithograph. 1896.

Fig. 2. OSVALD'S BREAKDOWN. Lithograph. 1920.

Fig. 3. OMEGA AND THE FLOWERS. Lithograph. 1908–9.

Long since extinguished now the sun's triumphal pyre;
Thundering breakers hurl the spars of fury
To the muffled drums of the storm:

> Borne in your chariot of steel
> Across the molten wastes,
> Fanned by the fiery breath of the clouds,
> Descend to us
> With savage smile
> And scorching breath!

From *Verwandlungen*

It is as though Shakespeare and Stefan George joined hands in this painting. And so it is understandable that the circle of poets with whom Munch associated in Germany at this time – Richard Dehmel, Stanislaw Przybyszewski, August Strindberg (Plate 26) – had more to offer him in his search for fresh content than the painters could offer. His friendship with the dramatist Gunnar Heiberg had already opened his mind to the realm of poetry. Above all his contact with Strindberg, whom he now met for the first time in person, gave a decisive stimulus to his intellectual development which persisted until his second Paris period. This does not imply that Munch accepted all and gave nothing in return. Strindberg had just published *Confession of a Fool* and was reaching out from an implacable realism to a new idealism, to the belief in those superior powers of light and inferior powers of darkness which intervene in men's lives and determine their fate. From the portrayal of human life he progressed to the treatment of fundamental, general, and perennially human problems in figures embodying some typical quality constantly recurring in all situations of life. The eternal legality of the ethical code replaces the rationalistic social portrayal of the age of Positivism. And the daemonic elements, drawn from the author's own experience, became here the primary object of consideration. This new note was first sounded in the short stories *Tschandala* and *By the Open Sea*. The aristocratic, creative male principle of the intellectual is undermined by the sub-human powers of evil. Strindberg's pessimistic attitude to life sees the female element, inasmuch as it is not maternal and subordinated to man, as the tool of daemonic powers. Woman is assigned a tragic intermediate position between the powers of good and evil; she is a figure of light or a daemon, often both. This conception, fundamentally medieval and spiritualist, was handed down to Strindberg and indeed to Munch as a legacy of Nordic pietism. Like Strindberg, Munch, too, was basically a solitary who never shook off his family heredity and to whom woman meant the seductive lure of the

17

daemonic. Thus Munch formulated these themes in his painting even before his contact with Strindberg. On the contrary, Strindberg, in his subsequent literary treatment of these themes as they appear most clearly in his Chamber Plays and Fairy Dramas, was probably influenced by the world of the painter.

During his years in Berlin Munch began to be active as a graphic artist, first in dry-point work, then in monochrome and colour lithographs and finally in woodcuts. Although he was completely self-taught in this field, apart from occasional advice from artist friends, he became one of the greatest masters of our century. Here, too, his development is characterized by gradual simplification and comprehension until it attains to a monumental grandeur. Many of his prints are remodellings of paintings: *The Sick Child, Summer Night* (*The Voice*, Plate 22), *The Kiss*. The modifications of the latter composition are indicative. In the relatively naturalistic etching of 1895 (Plate 28) the lovers are standing naked in the darkness in front of a window looking out on to a lighted street – the theme of the painting *Night* is continued. The measure of Munch's success in concentration of expression by means of progressive elimination of detail may be gauged from a woodcut version (Plate 29) made in Paris a few years later. It is a print made from two blocks. The group is fused into *one* great expressive symbol. Only the absolutely indispensable lines and surfaces were retained; the rest was dropped. The 'poster style' has reached perfection.

The shadows of mortality, the tragedy of death implicit in birth, darken Munch's portrayal of love. And so it is always surrounded by an atmosphere of darkness, death, and grief, like guilt and the Fall of Man with their implications of atonement. The end looms ahead even in the moment of greatest bliss. The painting *Ashes* (Plate 24) portrays man and woman after the Fall. He cowers in one corner of the picture, broken, lack-lustre, melting away into a trunk of the sombre pine forest that runs round to the front of the picture like a frame. She is shown full face, triumphant, regaining her composure yet infinitely poignant as she stands with arms flung back behind her head with its streaming locks as if in a gesture of silent despair, her gaze spanning time until she perceives the end.

One of Munch's most magnificent pictorial ideas is *Madonna* which portrays a woman at the moment of the sublimest ecstasy of love – the moment of conception. Munch carried out his idea first as a painting, then (1895/1902) as a lithograph (Plate 33) in black, blue, and dusky red which traces a glowing halo around the head. We recognize the broad, bold undulating movement of *The Cry*; it translates into visual terms the sensation of floating through the universe. The eyes are closed.

The pale face is framed in raven-black hair. It is an ecstatic countenance of almost unearthly beauty, but death is in that face.

In Paris Munch had already produced a fresh version of the theme of *Jealousy* (Plate 31) and had also made a lithograph of it. The imaginative background to this picture derives from the painter's personal experiences in Strindberg's circle in Berlin, linked up with the marriage between the Polish poet Przybyszewski and Dagny Juell (Plate 32), the Norwegian girl who inspired Strindberg's *Aspasia*. That Munch first painted this picture in Paris is shown by the fact that his model for the jealous man is the engraver Paul Herrmann, who states himself that he first became acquainted with Munch in Paris. In 1897 Munch painted Herrmann and his French friend Contard, a physician, in the strange double portrait (Plate 30) in the Kunsthistorisches Museum, Vienna; a picture uniting two contrasting types in the way he was fond of doing later with his models (as in *Dark and Fair* 1903). In the painting *Jealousy* in the Rasmus Meyer Collection all specific, temporal detail has disappeared, leaving only the enduringly human situation. Woman, the sinner, naked but for a red veil, the branches of the tree of knowledge encircling her like an ornament, irresistibly draws the stranger towards her with her floating tresses, while the man she has deceived, a pitiable figure crushed beneath his weight of anxiety, stares straight ahead, green in the face, aware of what is happening without needing to look. That undulating line of 'Art Nouveau' here becomes the perfect instrument of an art that probes the uttermost depths of the soul.

The historic relationship between Strindberg and Munch was strictly speaking the interaction of two closely related minds expressing themselves through differing artistic media. On the occasion of Munch's Paris exhibition Strindberg composed brief descriptions of his paintings, which Munch himself called 'Poems in prose': they were published in the *Revue Blanche* of June 1st, 1896.

THE EDVARD MUNCH EXHIBITION

Quelque incompréhensibles que soient
vos paroles, elles ont des charmes
BALZAC–*Séraphita*

Edvard Munch, aged thirty-two, the esoteric painter of love, jealousy, death, and sadness, has often been the victim of the deliberate misrepresentations of the executioner-critic who does his work with detachment and, like the public executioner, receives so much per head.

He has come to Paris to be understood by the initiate, with no fear of dying of the mockery which destroys cowards and weaklings but which, like a shaft of sunlight, lends a new brilliance to the shield of the valiant.

It has been said that music should be composed on Munch's paintings for their true interpretation. That may be so, but in the absence of a composer I shall provide the commentary on this group of pictures so reminiscent of Swedenborg's visions in the rapturous wisdom of conjugal love and the voluptuous folly of sensual love.

The Kiss. The fusion of two beings, the smaller of which, shaped like a carp, seems on the point of devouring the larger as is the habit of vermin, microbes, vampires, and women.

Alternatively: Man gives, creating the illusion that woman gives in return. Man begging the favour of giving his soul, his blood, his liberty, his repose, his eternal salvation, in exchange for what? In exchange for the happiness of giving his soul, his blood, his liberty, his repose, his eternal salvation.

Red Hair. A shower of gold falling on a despairing figure kneeling before his worse self and imploring the favour of being stabbed to death with her hairpin. Golden ropes binding him to earth and to suffering. Rain of blood falling in torrents over the madman in quest of unhappiness, the divine unhappiness of being loved, or rather of loving.

Jealousy. Jealousy, the sacred awareness that one's soul is one's own, that it abhors being mingled with another man by woman's agency. Jealousy, a legitimate egoism, born of the instinct to preserve the self and the race.

The jealous man says to his rival: 'Away with you, worthless fellow; you will warm yourself at fires I have kindled; you will inhale my breath from her lips; you will suck my blood and remain my slave, for you will be ruled by my spirit through this woman, who has become your master.'

Conception. Immaculate or not, it comes to the same thing: the red or gold halo crowns the accomplishment of the act, the sole end and justification of this creature devoid of existence in her own right.

The Scream. A scream of terror in the presence of nature flushed with anger and about to speak through storm and thunder to the petty hare-brained creatures posing as gods but without a godlike appearance.

Twilight. The sunlight fades, night falls, and twilight changes mortals into ghosts and corpses as they return home to envelop themselves in the shroud of their beds and to drift off into sleep. A seeming death which recreates life, a faculty of suffering, originating in either heaven or hell.

20

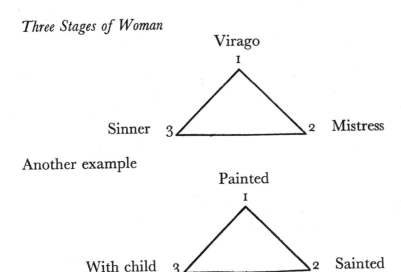

Three Stages of Woman

Virago
1

Sinner 3   2 Mistress

Another example

Painted
1

With child 3   2 Sainted

The Shore. The waves have snapped the tree-trunks but underground the roots are still alive, creeping along the dry sand to drink at the everlasting spring of their mother the sea! And the moon rises like the dot on an 'i', completing the melancholy and infinite desolation.

Venus rising from the waves and Adonis coming down from the mountains and villages. They make a pretence of watching the sea for fear of drowning in a look which will annihilate the self and merge them both in an embrace in which Venus becomes partly Adonis, and Adonis partly Venus.

AUGUST STRINDBERG

It may be recalled that Strindberg was asked by Gauguin a year earlier to write an introduction to the catalogue of his auction at Drouot's. Strindberg declined in a letter in which he tried to set forth the reasons for his refusal. This letter betrayed such a deep understanding of the essence of Gauguin's art that Gauguin had it printed at the head of his catalogue, together with his own letter in reply.

When Munch wrote poetry himself and illustrated it, he was following in Strindberg's footsteps. This is the case with the delightful cycle *Alpha and Omega* composed in 1908–9, a legend in the spirit of the Swedish author. Alpha represents the masculine principle. Omega is the temptress who approaches Alpha touchingly like a child, becomes his lover on the lonely island but deceives him with every animal living upon it. Omega is described as follows: 'Her eyes were changeable; on some days they were light blue but when she gazed upon her beloved they turned black with a carmine-red spark, and then she would sometimes conceal her mouth behind a flower' (Fig. 3). In the end she flies across the sea with the reindeer to the island beneath the moon, while Alpha, sunk in gloom, is surrounded by little bastards of snakes, bears, tigers, apes, pigs, and cats who call him 'father'. One day Omega returns and Alpha, with savage justice, slays her. In death her face resumes the child-like expression of their first encounter. Then all the animals fall upon Alpha and kill him, thus becoming sole masters of the island.

Two splendid self-portraits mark the end of the Berlin period. The painting *Self-portrait with a Cigarette* (Plate 27) dated 1895 is a vision of daemonic grandeur. The artist is shown lit from below. The richly pictorial treatment of the face and of the masterly hand shows how little Munch fell a prey to the danger of mere stylization. The great *painter* in Munch always has the decisive word. The picture seems to conclude Munch's 'blue period': apart from the reddish-yellow flesh the whole picture seems composed of varying shades of blue, blue-green, lilac, and violet. It is the vision of a man set in a blazing inferno of magic flames. This idea is not only a metaphorical interpretation, but was actually present to the painter's imagination, as is shown by another version of the same year, in which the artist, though treated far less as a portrait, stands naked in the same posture and with similar lighting in a ghostly no man's land. Munch called this picture *In Hell*. But the artist's spirit triumphs over hell, just as he triumphed over death. The second important self-portrait of this period is a lithograph: a pale, spiritual countenance (Plate 35) is seen full-face against a black background. The arm of a whitened skeleton lies in front of it like a barrier as if trying to cut off the artist from this world and claim him for the next. Munch, in whose family tuberculosis was a hereditary disease, had frequent struggles against death in his early years. This lithograph acts as a reminder of that fact. The pale man he portrays seems already to be greeting us from another world. Yet here, too, dominates the expression of the victorious immortality of the spirit. This theme in this setting reminds one of German artists' portraits with the figure of Death which can be traced from Burgkmair and Niklaus Manuel to Böcklin. Munch later returned to this idea in an etching of himself alongside a skeleton.

The year 1896 finds Munch in Paris again. The stylistic movement known as 'Art Nouveau' was at its culminating point and the appreciation of the Scandinavian artist was general. French art had continued to develop along the same lines. The new idealism prevailed also in poetry. Munch made a lithograph portrait of *Mallarmé* (Plate 34) and was accepted by his circle. He was regarded as a symbolist and neo-romantic like Maeterlinck. Strindberg was living in Paris about this time, undergoing a painful rebirth into a new piety, a new Christianity in the spirit of Swedenborg. He withdrew into a misanthropic and anguished solitude, avoiding even Munch, though he wrote the introduction and commentary quoted above to his exhibition. These were the years he described in his book *Inferno*. In 1896 Munch made a lithograph portrait of Strindberg; one can read in those features the same painful tension as in Munch's self-portrait already described. Munch's exhibition included pictures from earlier years in which the idea of the cyclic *Frieze of Life* emerges more and more clearly – the idea of a unified series of pictures to which would belong all his paintings dealing with the deepest problems of human existence.

These years proved particularly fertile for Munch as a graphic artist. The graphic arts, first of all lithography, experienced a brilliant renaissance in Paris during the nineties. The *Revue Blanche* was launched, with the collaboration of the 'Nabis' Vuillard, Bonnard, and Vallotton, and above all of Toulouse-Lautrec. This fresh ascendancy of lithography was made possible by 'Art Nouveau' and its emphasis on the significance of surface and pattern. In particular, colour lithography attained to the utmost perfection and refinement. Vuillard's prints produce the effect of precious tapestries in subdued colours. The extraordinary technical mastery of the lithographic printer Clot, who printed Toulouse-Lautrec's most beautiful lithographs, furthered this development. Munch brought a passionate interest to these new possibilities. He mixed his colours like an alchemist and was constantly inventing fresh refinements and variants which he dictated to his printer with closed eyes as he created in his imagination the vision of the completed work. Such was the origin of that splendid print, *The Sick Child* (Plate 37), a monumental enhancement of the main figure of his earlier picture. Munch's undulating lines are seen in the hair playing round the infinitely moving profile of a being rendered more beautiful through its spiritualization when dying. The way in which the skin tautly stretched over the bones conveys the sensation of wasting away with seizing directness.

At that time Toulouse-Lautrec was the dominant artistic figure. Although differing completely from Munch in character and temperament he does display a certain affinity with him in his pessimism and his ruthless portrayal of the abysses of the human soul. Moreover, the impression made on Munch by Toulouse-Lautrec's matchless feeling for style and his ingenious draughtsmanship should not be underestimated. An example of this is a cover drawing made by Toulouse-Lautrec for a programme of the Théâtre Libre, which was connected with the Revue Blanche; it illustrates Fabre's comedy *L'Argent*. Compare the powerful impact of this black and white drawing executed with a bare minimum of means, with the final version of Munch's *Kiss*, made in 1897. Both rest on the same principle of expressive surface pattern. For the same theatre Munch designed the programme for Ibsen's *Peer Gynt*.

Between 1896 and 1899 Munch had made lithographs of a series of his own paintings, connected thematically with the *Frieze of Life*, intending to publish them as a cycle. The cycle was in fact never published, but to this project we owe graphic versions of Munch's pictorial ideas which are concentrated, simplified, and enhanced in expression. One of these is the lithograph *Anxiety* whose painted version was made in 1894 (Plate 18). The idea goes back to the pale, ghostly figures in *Karl-Johan Street* and is combined with the scenery of *The Cry*. The background is a similar landscape of Nordic fjords with carmine-red clouds extending high above people of death-like pallor. They are all shown full-face, staring straight ahead. They stand there side by side, oddly aloof yet all transfixed by the same crippling fear as if by an evil spell which blots out their features, leaving only luminous bright discs.

The lithograph *Chamber of Death* (Fig. 1) also goes back to a painting (see note to Plate 20) from the *Frieze of Life*. The people in the sick-room are bowed down beneath their weight of sorrow during the last moments of someone they love. We cannot see the dying girl, who is sitting in a wicker chair, but we can read what is happening in the grief-stricken faces of her relatives. The groups of standing and sitting figures and the young man merge with the sick-bed into one dark mass and yet retain their separate identity – the effect is tremendous. The old father is praying, a woman is arranging the pillow, a brother stands at the window to hide his tears. Once more we encounter the rapidly foreshortened perspective which in itself arouses a feeling of alienation, abandonment, and helpless surrender. The female figure seen full-face has Inger's features, and it is not difficult to trace again the source of the inspiration in Munch's own experience in his family circle on the death of his sister. The same dark anxiety pervades this work as inspires Strindberg's later dramas *Sheet-Lightning*, *Ghost Sonata*, *Scene of Conflagration*, and *At the Stake*.

Another death-bed scene of 1895 (Rasmus Meyer Collection) shows the dying girl lying in bed sharply foreshortened, a device already used in the art of former centuries to express man's helplessness in death.

Only the wasted hands writhing in the death agony reveal that a spark of life still flickers within her. The lithograph (Plate 36) which repeats this composition shows the dying girl's vision – faces rising from the waves and disappearing again, a reminder of what is past, and a presage of what is to come. Thus she lies in bed as though in a skiff about to push off from the bank while those remaining are strung out one behind the other in rapidly dwindling perspective as if on the river bank, each one reacting to the event in his own way: one is praying, quiet, and composed, another is crumpled up with grief, another is sunk in dull helpless reverie. And again that tall, tragic female figure reminiscent of Inger dominates the foreground. The enormous vitality of this compositional arrangement is shown by the fact that Munch recast it in yet another version in 1915 with different mourners drawn from those vigorous human types which were the fruits of his new trend towards realism, but he lost none of its tragic urgency. But the most deeply moving of Munch's pictures of death is *The Dead Mother* (Plate 48) in the Kunsthalle, Bremen (1899–1900). Its subject is a little girl who has just turned away from the bed where she has been to looking for her mother. Now the last breath of life has left the poor decaying mortal frame, and her mother has gone for ever. The little girl is running away, unwilling to take in the full horror of it, as children often do when trying to ward off some nightmarish terror. The little face is not yet distorted with grief as in the gruesome etching of 1901, but rather unmoved, with big round eyes and even a slightly stupid expression – the embarrassed look children have when uncertain what they should do. It is no use crying, for she is really quite alone; there is no-one to hear or comfort her. She would like to run away, but away from what, and where to? So she raises her arms as if to shut her ears to the fearful stillness around her, in that eternal gesture Munch gives to women in the presence of death. In this immobile childish face is born the presentiment of something so appalling that she cannot and will not grasp it, but merely feels that it is inevitable. An adult at such moments is said to be 'turned to stone'. It is a measure of Munch's ineffably profound humanity that he could communicate this quite clearly in the soft face of a child, too young to be 'turned to stone'.

Themes such as these make up the *Frieze of Life*. Munch exhibited it in 1902 in the Berlin Secession. Pictures of life on one side were matched by pictures of death on the other. As early as 1889 Munch wrote in his journal: 'We should stop painting interiors with people reading and women knitting. We should create living people who breathe and feel and suffer and love – I shall paint a series of such pictures. People

25

will understand the sanctity of the theme and remove their hats as they do in church.'

When Munch exhibited the *Frieze of Life* in Kristiania in 1918 he provided the public with the following printed statement: 'I have worked on this Frieze, with long intervals, for close on thirty years. The first rough draft dates back to 1888–9. *The Kiss*, the so-called *Yellow Boat*, *The Street*, *Man and Wife*, and *Anxiety* were painted between 1890 and 1891, and on view here in this city in the Tostrupgården and later in the same year at my Berlin exhibition. The following year fresh works were added to the series, including *Vampire*, *The Cry*, and *Madonna*, and it was exhibited as an independent Frieze in a private gallery on the Unter-den-Linden. These pictures were exhibited in 1902 (in fact February 1904, cf. J. Thiis, *Munch*, Oslo 1933, p. 215) in the Berlin Secession, where they were displayed as a continuous frieze all round the imposing entrance hall, as examples of modern psychic life. They were later shown at Blomquist's in 1903 and 1909. Certain art critics have sought to prove that the thought content of this Frieze was influenced by German ideas and my acquaintance with Strindberg; I trust that the foregoing comments will suffice to refute this assertion. . . . The Frieze was conceived as a series of decorative pictures which would collectively present a picture of life. They are traversed by the indented coastline; beyond lies the ever-restless sea, and under the tree-tops is life in all its fulness, its variety, its joys and its sorrows.'

Munch could provide ocular demonstration of this idea of a Frieze of Life only for short periods during exhibitions. Not until later life was he given the opportunity to carry out his idea as a unity, in the wall paintings of the canteen for the employees of the Freia chocolate factory in Oslo, this time only in the concise aphoristic form in which the ageing master was able to cast this monumental task.

One of the most important pictures of this Frieze of Life is *Three Stages of Woman* (Plate 38) of which he made a lithograph in 1899. The themes are Maiden, Prostitute, and Mother – love unfolding, love consuming, and love consumed. The wavy coastline motif intended to run through all the outdoor scenes of the cycle to represent the common bond of the sea linking all life together, is of particular importance here. Not merely the figures but the empty spaces too are eloquent – this is even clearer in the lithograph than in the painting. The white empty spaces turn into daemonic beings groping for and clinging to the women. The *Three Stages of Woman* inspired one of the most beautiful of Egon Schiele's larger works (unfortunately since destroyed): *The Three Mothers*. As with Munch the middle figure was naked and consumed with inner fire like a furnace; she was pregnant. At her right

26

stood the figure entitled 'Dying Fires': she held her child in her arms, her eyes shining. At her left stood the figure 'Consumed' who had dropped her child – she was dead.

THE WORLD OF REALITY

THE YEARS FOLLOWING the second Paris period were spent travelling from place to place – mainly in Germany but including trips to France and Italy. But Munch returned constantly to his native Scandinavia, which remained his deepest source of inspiration for the portrayal of man and nature. From 1900 onwards portraiture and landscape took up more and more space in Munch's work. This resulted in a new fusion of both, as in the days of his Impressionistic beginnings. The double portrait *Mother and Daughter* (Plate 39) in the Oslo National Gallery is an impressive monument to this endeavour; it is one of the wisest, simplest, most monumental of Munch's pictures painted at the close of the century. The figures are set against a Nordic landscape in the bright moonlight of a summer night. The mother, in dark clothes, is seated; the daughter, in light clothes, is standing. The undulating lines of the coastal scenery unite the figures with the background, and yet they free themselves again from it through their fluid, vibrant outlines. The descending dark silhouette of the wood repeats the cadence of the mother's figure. And then the rafters of a wooden roof project in a straight line to provide a foil to the daughter's shoulders as she stands there in her starched linen dress like a soldier on parade. The mother on the other hand needs no support – in fact she supports the earth seething round her in dark shapeless lines and masses. A pale moon rises between the two figures. The mother's face gleams through the darkness in the moon's borrowed light, while in the shadows her daughter's face, sunburnt but deprived of its rights like the vanished daylight, stands out in dark relief against a light background. The matriarchal idea could not be expressed with greater simplicity, or more telling force: the old one withdrawing into the shadows to make way for the younger, brighter, lighter figure, but in appearance only, for she retains the power; her wish and will penetrate everything with a magic force. She is the life-giver and yet something of the power of death sits in her face.

It is astonishing to see Munch in this picture returning to the world of reality from the land of dreams, symbols, and visions, but without forfeiting to the world of the senses that visionary power he had learnt to master.

Munch's experience gained with figure composition was subsequently turned to good account in landscape painting. The motifs are taken mainly from the fjord landscape and the Oslo archipelago but are divested of all descriptive rendering of locality. The bright, moonlit night of the Scandinavian winter is a favourite theme of the landscapes Munch painted at the turn of the century. The painting in the Mannheim Kunsthalle shows the *Oslo Fjord* as seen from Nordstrand. A long tapering island is reflected in the dark water, and this double image becomes a mouth with soft, full lips, animated like a living creature, mysterious as a symbol (Plate 42).

From being renderings of definite aspects of reality, the paintings are gradually reduced to the great, eternally valid rhythms of nature. It is a fairy tale wood simply, beneath its mantle of snow, which faces the onlooker in the picture painted in 1899 (National Gallery, Oslo; Plate 43). In the painting dated 1901 entitled *White Night* (Plate 47) the same curves are used to delineate the trees wrapped in their winter sleep and the sea caught in the iron grip of the ice. Circles of light shine like stars in the firmament and glow like mysterious fires in the dark branches of the fir-trees. Never before has a painter conveyed so impressively the enchantment and sublime poetry of a Nordic winter's night. Landscapes like these are renderings of an inner vision prompted by actual contact with nature. 'You cannot paint pictures like these from nature,' declared the artist, 'you must draw such pictures from your inner self.' And also the long, light nights of the Scandinavian summer transform the landscape so as to disclose its 'second sight'. This process begins with *Mystic of a Summer Night* (1892), is intensified in *Moonlit Night* of 1895 (Mustad Collection, Oslo), and culminates in the majestic *Summer Night at the Shore* (Plate 45) in the Kunsthistorisches Museum, Vienna.

Trees, houses, and people are caught up in the great rhythm of the lines and surfaces. In 1900 Munch painted a group of girls standing on a jetty at dusk (Plate 44). Here the alarmingly rapid foreshortening has assumed the soft, friendly character of a longing and yearning for distant horizons. Munch's saying: 'Art is crystallization' reveals the entire significance of his creative activity. He found it hard to part from his pictures, and kept most of them at home. Exhibitions of his works made him uneasy. He needed to be constantly surrounded by his pictorial ideas which he was always developing further, always recasting in fresh, simpler, more monumental forms. In the second version of

28

Girls on a Jetty (Plate 46) he extended the motif. We see the majestic dome of the large tree reflected in the water, which was also used separately by Munch as the subject of a landscape painting. The group of girls becomes anonymous; stripped of all individuality, they are mere emotive points of emphasis in the light summer night. Simplification implies intensification. The same scenery reappears in a painting of 1903: this time the movement in space is centralized, anchored to the almost ceremonially impressive group of girls surrounding the towering figure of the woman painter Aase Nørregaard. With their light colours they are contrasted with a darker element, a compact group of men staring in silence at the water. The total effect is of a symphony in flamingo pink and carmine red, expressive of the bland warmth of the evening.

After formulating the basic compositional ideas which combined in his mind to form the *Frieze of Life*, Munch turned increasingly to landscape painting, and also to portraits of people, singly or in groups. In the Berlin period and the second Paris period he endeavoured to elaborate varying intellectual types. Hence his subjects do not always avoid the danger of a certain typification. (This is true, for example, of the portraits of Strindberg.) But now Munch is far more receptive to the impact of the individual personality, thus achieving most striking representations of people, particularly in the graphic arts. About 1898 he painted Ibsen in the Café of the Grand-Hotel at Kristiania (Plate 40); in 1902 he made a magnificent lithograph of the same subject. From the shadow-filled room one looks out onto Karl-Johan Street, dreary beneath the pelting rain. The bright face of the poet, framed in gleaming white hair, blazes like a Saint Elmo's fire or like a star in this world of Nordic twilight: a light-giver of compelling majesty. (In another lithograph Munch superimposed this face like a mask upon the beams of light radiating from the lantern of a light-house.) His body is entirely ignored; only the curious pentagonal head is visible. Even so, the outline of the body is hinted at by the dark background of the curtain whose curves fall parallel to the figure. *One* shape is firmly anchored in the other. There are no vacua. What in other pictures is neutral, meaningless, empty space is for Munch a living creature playing its part in the picture as a whole. The painter could not break free from Ibsen's world. In 1906 he was commissioned by Max Reinhardt to make the décor for *Ghosts*. He portrayed the onset of Osvald's illness (Fig. 2) in a harrowing lithograph and also in 1920 he painted an interior for the concluding tableau of this play.

The magnificent head of the violinist Eva Mudocci (1903; Plate 50), framed by her wavy locks as by an ornament, contrives to suggest by means of the slender neck the tall, imposing, majestic figure of its subject. (Munch also made a lithograph of her playing a violin and piano duet with her accompanist.) This lithograph is a masterly example of the way in which Munch, despite the highly decorative effect of his work, permits nothing meaningless, every stroke standing in a spiritual relation to the whole. Dark tongues of flame leap out of her hair, mysterious eyes peer out, even the brooch acquires a face. It is a recurrence of the theme of *Madonna*, but this Madonna, instead of being consumed in daemonic flames, has by her spiritual power overcome and sublimated the daemonic fire: she is an artist. The result is one of the most splendid, most spiritualized female portraits ever created.

As Munch developed further so he devoted himself more and more to woodcuts. For these he employed not cross-cut timber but long-cut timber. Resistance of his medium fired him with enthusiasm; the tougher the wood the better. He does not eliminate its natural structure but allows it full play in the rough surfaces of his design. His woodcuts thereby acquire an original power and primitive grandeur far surpassing the spiritual intensity of the paintings. *The Primitive Man* (1905; Plate 51) portrays the head and shoulders of an old sailor. Those who see in Munch's art and human types a Viking quality, something proceeding from the very depths of the Nordic soul, find strong support for this view in a work such as this. At the same time it is a conception of humanity of that moving objectivity and inner grandeur first introduced into modern art by Van Gogh. These woodcuts, like the lithographs, are often printed from plates of extraordinary dimensions.

Munch, in his double portrait of Herrmann and Contard, sought to combine two contrasting human types in one picture. In the portrait of his friends Aase and Harald Nørregaard, a married couple (Oslo, National Gallery), he portrayed the profound and tranquil harmony uniting two human souls without infringing their separate existence within their own independent personalities. This juxtaposition of a pure profile and an austere full-face recalled to Jens Thiis – quite justifiably – the Venetian portraits of the Renaissance. One would also agree with Thiis when he attributes to Velazquez the stimulus to life-size male portraits which Munch took up particularly during the first decade of the new century. Munch studied the great Spaniard's works in the Louvre, as is evident from the early portrait of the painter Jensen-Hjell (1885). But these impressions had long been assimilated and recast in his own artistic terms. Munch knew the great power of expression his line possessed. He always set his subjects against a light background so that in their dark, modern men's clothing their very outline acquired the utmost eloquence and revealed their whole character. Face and hands betray no more than has been stated by the figure as a whole. In the portrait of the French-Swiss Archimard (Plate 52), a writer, the outline is supremely eloquent, revealing the nervous, sophisticated, slightly neurotic character of the model, which the slender bony hands and the fine long head merely reaffirm. What a contrast with the self-assured, jovial bonhomie of Schlittgen, the cartoonist of the 'Fliegende Blätter,' German to the core with his sturdy reality and his air of bourgeois prosperity. Munch liked his pictures to be connected with each other. The idea of a higher cyclic unity never left him. And so he set these two against each other as a pair of contrasts: *The Frenchman – The German* (Plate 53) – an idea which certainly did not occur to him until the work was finished. It is amazing how much of the essential national character Munch has captured here, over and above the individual personality. With Munch the strong emphasis on space, which nonetheless has to harmonize with the surface area, always causes his figures to stand on a tilted base, so that they appear larger than life – a kind of conscious magnifying, or rather, exaggeration of the proportions. Thus his spare, long-limbed men – Helge Rode, Jappe Nilssen, (Plate 55) – stand on unusually large feet. The powerful figure of the Consul Sandberg (1901; Oslo, Kommunes Kunstsamlinger), like so many of the Pycnotype, has tiny feet and reminds one of the 'Colossus with feet of clay'. Even so, the canvas was not high enough to accommodate the whole figure, and the painter was obliged to add on a strip at the bottom.

This series of life-size male portraits also contains a self-portrait (Plate 54), the property of the city of Oslo. Although not one of his most popular works and rarely reproduced, it is nevertheless one of his most remarkable. It shows Munch full-face, his legs slightly apart, his body turned slightly to the right, but no longer as the Bohemian and fighter of the self-portraits painted during the Berlin period. He is wearing a long, cassock-like coat with a high collar, a really festive garment, and holds his brushes in his hand but no palette. This was certainly not the painter's habitual attire when working. On looking at this picture one falls victim to an optical illusion: the light streaks of the brushes appear to be the edge of a darkly bound volume he carries in his left hand – a Bible. It is the typical attitude of the Protestant divine as he appears before his flock, an attitude familiar to us in the portraits by Frans Hals and other Dutch masters. It is doubtful whether this effect was intentional. It might well have been the unconscious emergence of ancient family traditions which influenced the attitude adopted in this self-portrait. It is clear from this painting that

31

Munch saw the artist not merely as a Bohemian but also as teacher, admonisher and judge.

The problem of the group portrait had already occupied Munch in the 'eighties, when he painted his friends – lawyers and writers – Anker Hambro, Johan Collett Michelsen, and Knudsen grouped around a table in the cosy lamplight. After 1900 he took up this problem again.

In a picture painted in 1902, now in Stuttgart, Württembergische Staatsgalerie, he has caught and held four little girls he met in the streets of Åsgårdstrand (Plate 56). The tallest is leading by the hand the three others whose heads are graded down in steps. They stand out against a patch of damp snow and the brightly painted wall of a house; their circular and many-pointed caps frame their curly heads like haloes. Shivering, rather lonely, and sad, they were traversing this late winter landscape when they met the painter. One admires Munch's powers of interpreting the soul of a child, his ability to comprehend utterly each one of these human beings, anticipating their adult characters without destroying the wondering innocence of childhood. Each little soul remains self-contained and isolated, despite its feeling of interdependence – the eternal tragedy of mankind already expressed in this quartette.

An equally magnificent character study of a group of children is the picture of the four sons of the Lübeck ophthalmologist Dr. Max Linde (Plate 57). They too are dark figures standing out against a light double-door while the parquet, like a dark lake, reflects their figures in shimmering patches. How their characters unfold, part of them wrapped up in a dream, the other part keenly awake! They show the slight embarrassment of well-to-do children who are obliged to behave in accordance with their social status but who would rather be romping in the garden or the meadow. The smallest one as if seeking support and protection as best he may, snuggles close against his eldest brother, whose demeanour reveals his feeling of responsibility for the others, even though his thoughts seem to stray elsewhere.

Munch cherished the hope of realizing his *Frieze of Life* in the home of his Lübeck friend and Maecenas. Although this document of imagination never came into being, Munch did complete in the 'Linde-Folio' one of the most beautiful documents of reality, which portrays his friend's house, estate and family in masterly dry-point plates.

About the same time Munch painted the *Family on the Road* (Plate 49) in the Thielska Gallery, Stockholm. To this extraordinary picture, one of Munch's most sublime creations, too little consideration has

32

Fig. 4. FUNERAL MARCH. Lithograph. 1897.

Fig. 5. THE TRIAL BY FIRE. Woodcut. About 1927.

Fig. 6. DIGGERS ON THE ROAD. Lithograph. 1920.

Fig. 7. INTERIOR OF THE ASSEMBLY HALL OF THE UNIVERSITY OF OSLO.

been given so far. Three female figures, dressed in mourning, stand lonely on a road which crosses a deserted autumnal countryside. The eye of the artist has caught them on their way to visit relatives or friends. They stop for a moment, but the moment turns to eternity. The psychical interpretation of the three stages of woman – of the budding child, the young mother, struck by the first great dolour of her life, and the ageing one for whom life declines – is unsurpassed. They look as if they had lost their fathers and supporters. Munch has interpreted this with incredible delicacy and subtlety, rendering the spiritual essence of each of the three.

The time of origin is assumed to be 1903, quite plausible if we compare Plates 56, 57. As they stand there, these figures of everyday life grow up to mythical grandeur like the Norns of the Scandinavian sagas. Munch liked this kind of gradation of characters as shown before in the *Three Stages of Woman* (Plate 38) and in the *Dance of Life*, Oslo, National Gallery (Thiis p. 261). By applying to the group *one* waving outline, the artist has stressed its surface values and monumentality.

Art historians who have analysed Munch's work have established that in 1907 his style of painting underwent a change. The ornamental, stylized, graphic element in his forms gives way to a looser style in which the structure of each single brush-stroke once more comes into its own. The designer's habit of leaving parts of the canvas bare disappears, the smoothly blended manner is replaced by thick applications of paint. This was seen as a divergence from the ideals of his youth and an approach to a certain degree of Naturalism or even Impressionism. This style is seen not only in his compositions with figures, in which nude studies are assigned a particularly important role. Already in *Death of Marat* (Oslo, Kommunes Kunstsamlinger) and in the two interiors, so reminiscent of Bonnard's, *Girl at the Window* and *Girl Dressing* (all three done in 1906) this new brushwork is evident. In 1907 it appears in the double nude study of two slender girls (Oslo, Kommunes Kunstsamlinger, Hodin 74) and in the *Yellow Nude*, also in the various versions of the theme of *Amor and Psyche*. These latter show a male and a female nude standing or sitting facing each other, the man embracing the woman (*Consolation*; Hodin 49). Broad bands of colour run down like shimmering streams of rain so that the picture appears to vibrate. We encounter the same style of painting in his landscapes, from which I should like to single out *House with a Red Roof* (Glaser, Fig. 47) and *Luebeck Harbour with Steamer* (Plate 59; both done in 1907) because of their superb quality. Gone are the ornamental interlacing and fusion in the picture surface. Each brush-stroke is laden with spatial and formal significance and suggests the picture's successive depths. Their unison produces a most powerful effect of atmosphere: the landscapes seem bathed in light.

Finally, the life-size full-length portrait also takes part in this development and we find in this category examples ranging from 1906 to 1910: Ludwig Karsten, Count Kessler and Ernest Thiel 1906, Helge Rode 1908, Dr. Daniel Jacobsen (Plate 60), Jappe Nilssen, Thorwald Stang and Jens Thiis 1909, Christian Gierløff 1910. The brush-strokes run diagonally so that one is reminded of the street pictures of the first Paris period, but the diagonal lines no longer run all the same way but in contrary directions so that the picture, despite all its vibrant quality, acquires a crystalline solidity hitherto unknown.

It is wrong to speak of Impressionism in this context. The elemental glow of the colours is intensified in a way which has nothing in common with Impressionism. Not only is it communicated to the entire surface of the canvas but it clings to every stroke of the brush. The self-portrait Munch painted in the sanatorium in Copenhagen (Plate 61; 1909), shows the artist sitting by the open window through which brilliant light penetrates; the deep luminous blue of his jacket is a loosely woven fabric of single brush-strokes. If a parallel is to be sought elsewhere it can only be found in the paintings of Van Gogh. This apparent Impressionism is in fact an enhanced Expressionism.

SYNTHESIS

THE YEAR 1908–9 brought a crisis in the artist's life. His restless, roving existence, with but short intervals of stay in Norway, led to a serious nervous breakdown which overtook him in Copenhagen on his way home. He spent several months in Doctor Jacobsen's private clinic for nervous diseases, during which he nevertheless went on with his work as a painter. Some of his finest portraits were painted in these surroundings. Thus Munch's development suffered no interruption or change, for the decisive turning-point had already occurred in 1907.

After this crisis, which lasted for six months, the painter returned to Norway. There he settled and thereafter made only occasional trips abroad. He had already written in a letter: 'Norway, whither I shall surely return one day, for her natural beauty is important enough for my art.' Munch returned to his native soil restored to health and vigour and having attained a greater maturity. He acquired a house and land set in Norway's magnificent fjord and island scenery, first on Kragerø and Skrubben, then in Ramme near Hvidsten, in Grimsrød on Jelø, and finally in the earthly paradise of Ekely, the last of his homes. Munch became a farmer who owned horses, geese, hens and dogs, discovering in these creatures and their keepers fresh material for his art, and embarking upon a more intense and direct portrayal of nature. His study of the nude received fresh impetus: human bodies enveloped in the atmosphere of the shimmering sea and radiant beneath the Scandinavian sun, overflowing with light and health, now entered his pictures. This development became the basis for an attempt in monumental painting. During his stay in the house of his friend Dr. Linde in Luebeck Munch had become acquainted with the great winged altar-pieces of the Gothic masters in churches and museums there. Now he ventured upon a similar task, but within the framework of his own modern idiom. Between the years 1907 and 1913 he painted a triptych showing men bathing (Plate 58). It is not a simple Impressionist picture of a beach with bathers, but again a kind of Frieze of Life showing youth, maturity, and age, with figures in monumentally enhanced attitudes, running their course in obedience to a mighty law. This urge to the monumental which repeatedly breaks through was to find its ultimate fulfilment in the artist's mature years.

It was already stated at the beginning that the three European painters exercising a decisive influence on the evolution in style which took place around 1900, namely Hodler, Klimt, and Munch, regarded monumental undertakings as the real goal of their activity. It was their tragedy that the age in which they lived did not encourage this lofty aim, the realization of which was repeatedly frustrated and only achieved after bitter struggles. The ideal outcome of these efforts would have been the fresco. It was granted to only one of the three, Hodler, to achieve this aim in a museum of historic style little suited to it: *The Retreat from Marignano* in the Armour Hall of the Landesmuseum in Zurich. Everything else remained fragmentary; vast canvases were dispersed here and there of which only two, *The Departure of the Students for War* in Jena and *Unanimity* in the Hanover Town Hall, arrived at the destination originally intended for them. Hodler came to Paris in 1891, at a time when Munch was also living there, and came into contact with the same artistic circles. If the exhibition at the Rosicrucians' Salon, initiated by Peladan, can be in any way regarded as an artistic event, it is solely because Hodler exhibited there his painting *Those Who are Weary of Life* for the first time. The fact that this picture later found its way into a Vienna collection (Reininghaus) is again

35

symptomatic. The great mutual esteem and friendship uniting Hodler and Klimt receives far too scant attention in the history of art. In 1904, at Klimt's instigation, Hodler, Munch, and Aksel Gallén (who exhibited in Berlin along with Munch that same year) were invited to exhibit their collected works in the Vienna Secession. In his beginnings, at the time of the building of the Vienna Ringstrasse with its historical architecture and of the Makart tradition, Klimt received commissions in plenty, including frescoes (Burgtheater, Kunsthistorisches Museum); but when he fashioned his own style in his maturer years his art met with resistance. His main work, the monumental ceiling paintings symbolizing *Philosophy* (1900), *Medicine* (1901), and *Jurisprudence* (1903) in the University of Vienna, was rejected by the College of Professors and found their way into a private collection which was destroyed during the recent war by retreating SS troops. Thus the most important achievement of this great artist can now be studied only in reproductions.

One can, in contrast to this, say that Munch was favoured by destiny in that his wall paintings for Oslo University did finally reach their intended destination, but only after bitter struggles and the painter's untiring efforts.

The idea of an embracing whole to which the artist's individual pictorial creations must be subordinated always dominated Munch's thought. It underlies the conception of the *Frieze of Life*, the idea of which pervades his whole work. He constantly cherished the hope of realizing it in the architectural unity of a representative hall and since such an opportunity never occurred he sought to realize this idea at least temporarily in exhibitions. Munch used the word 'decorative' to describe his artistic aims, whereas we should today employ the term 'monumental'. Hodler's and Klimt's endeavours both had this same underlying aim. The fact that there was, at last, a prospect of the concrete realization of this aim in the wall paintings for the University, fired the painter's enthusiasm.

The new Assembly Hall of the University, on which building was begun in 1909, was to be decorated with frescoes on the large wall areas, whereby due consideration should be given to the Hall's architecture in Greek style. Five artists were invited to compete, among them Munch. A jury which included the important fresco-painter Joakim Skovgaard and Jens Thiis, was to judge between the projects submitted. As was to be expected, only those of Munch possessed any artistic merit, though the original version had to undergo some modifications. The enigmatic *Mountain of Men*, showing the influence of Nietzsche's philosophy, formed the centre-piece; it was rejected by

36

Skovgaard and Thiis. The jury were quite right in their verdict upon the *Mountain of Men* and Munch showed wisdom in bowing to their decision on this point, yet this work does afford us a deep insight into Munch's art, discussed at length by the philosopher Gösta Svenaeus in a most serious and important book (see Bibliography). It examines with particular penetration one aspect of Munch's art hitherto intentionally neglected by scholars since it does not always concern his most powerful works; namely the metaphysical, speculative aspect. This aspect, however, does exist and to Svenaeus goes the credit for indicating its importance, even if one cannot follow all his bold philosophical conclusions. One feels that perhaps too much stress is laid on Nietzsche's influence – after all Munch himself rejected the alleged 'influence of German ideas' on his *Frieze of Life*. Nevertheless Munch strikes a note here whose existence cannot be denied. Its origin certainly lies as far back as the Paris years from 1889 to 1892 when Munch encountered a work as intellectually grandiose as it was artistically unfortunate, a work of the French sculptor who, in France alone, developed *art nouveau* to a kind of Expressionism: Rodin's *Gate of Hell*. Svenaeus rightly emphasized its influence on the original centre-piece of the University wall paintings, the *Mountain of Men* (Svenaeus p. 37); naked bodies wallowing in death and decay are piled high, forming an eery tower that strives to reach the light.

Meanwhile Munch had been in Germany. In Weimar he came into contact with the Nietzsche circle, made a portrait of the philosopher's sister Elisabeth and painted for the collector Ernest Thiel an ideal portrait of Nietzsche (Plate 63). In 1893, in a letter to Johan Rohde, he criticized German art unfavourably but admitted that a few artists were of such immense stature that they surpassed all the rest: Böcklin, Klinger, Thoma, Wagner, and Nietzsche. This world of ideas, which we are inclined today to associate rather with the tragedy of German painting, did by his own confession exert a strong influence on Munch. Thus there is no denying the ferment of *Zarathustra* in the *Mountain of Men*. The same idea is already apparent in the macabre lithograph *Funeral March* of 1897 (Fig. 4). Themes from Nietzsche's *Thus spake Zarathustra* are also encountered elsewhere in the unpublished artistic material Munch left behind at his death, e.g. the picture of the crucified man raised high above the crowd (Plate 62b).

The apex of the pyramid of bodies in the *Mountain of Men* was crowned by a radiant sun. In the final version in the Assembly Hall it is all that remained of the original idea. Munch, with his sound artistic instinct, had found his way back from Nietzsche to Van Gogh. The bodies of the *Mountain of Men* were dispersed but for a few who strayed

37

into the side panels flanking the main pictures to form groups which call to mind the noble, natural classicism of Hans von Marées rather than Nietzsche's Zarathustra myth.

But nothing which had once taken shape in Munch's artistic imagination disappeared from it entirely. Just as all Munch's artistic ideas persisted and periodically received fresh incarnations, so this *Mountain of Men* recurred too. Svenaeus pointed out that in the mid-twenties Munch took up again this idea of the *Mountain of Men* with renewed power and greater maturity and worked diligently at it, perhaps in the hope of being able to incorporate it in the monumental decorations planned for the new Town Hall (Plate 62a). In the first version Munch had used his *Madonna* as if it were a figure for a portal. There now appears in her place an enigmatic hermaphrodite creature, a sphinx with mighty breasts and Munch's own ageing, disillusioned features. Here lies the key to this immensely tragic and problematic work which was condemned by itself to remain a fragment. Yet this sphinx exercises a magic fascination. At its feet, like the caryatides of this strange mausoleum composed of human bodies, rise up slender female figures already familiar to us from the series of pictures: *The Day of a Model*. To the left of this second *Mountain of Men* was to extend – as the left wing – the landscape of *History*, not as a friendly setting for the old narrator but as the scene of a mad flight of naked human bodies reminiscent of Daumier's plastic relief *Les Emigrants*. The title *Storm* (Oslo, Kommunes Kunstsamlinger, Svenaeus p. 106) recalls the painting of 1893. The right wing was to portray a broad landscape spanned by a rainbow: a continuation of the 'sun' theme and a peaceful solution of torturing pessimism.

From the very beginning of these University wall paintings *History* was a decisive factor as the picture of a dignified old man seated at the foot of a centuries-old ash-tree in splendid fjord scenery, handing down tradition to a small boy by telling the sagas of the past. There was close competition between Munch and the painter Vigeland with the condition that by August, 1911, they should complete one or two full-size compositions which would then be affixed to the walls. Thiis tells us that Munch's fighting spirit instead of being broken by this condition was actually strengthened by it. He is said to have painted in all about twenty-three full-size pictures, so that he was able to confront the next meeting of the jury not merely with one or two paintings but with the complete cycle in the actual size required. Munch accompanied the completed work with a commentary for the jury classic in its lapidary style: 'I wished my decorations to form an independent realm of ideas, the image of which should be at the same time specifically Norwegian

38

and broadly human. As regards the Greek architectural style of the Hall I believe it has several points of contact with my style of painting, particularly in its simplification and treatment of flat areas, so that the Hall and the wall paintings "go together" decoratively, even if the pictures are Norwegian.' (Thiis p. 300.)

Thus Munch at last drew the final inference of his stylistic endeavour and his treatment of surface, by fitting it into an architectural whole. A work of genuine monumental painting was therewith created. He concentrated all his pictorial vigour on the three main panels – he intended them to appear 'weighty and imposing like massed bunches of flowers in the Hall'. The *Mountain of Men* had been replaced by the mighty painting of the *Sun* (Plate 64) rising over a sea and mountain scenery, the Norwegian Skaergaard. One can understand that it profoundly impressed Richard Strauss when conducting a symphony concert in the Hall, for there he was confronted with the content of the opening bars of his *Zarathustra* in terms of colour. It is a landscape of lofty grandeur and simplicity. Above it the miracle of flaming light shines in its architectonic austerity like the rose window of a medieval cathedral. It controls with solemn restraint the cosmic rays which blaze so destructively in Van Gogh's pictures of the sun. And this powerful, self-created light seems to be fashioning the very substance of the earth.

The right-hand panel, *Alma Mater* (Plate 66), was entitled in the original version *Explorers* (Plate 65b). Groups of young people were absorbed in the wonders of nature. They disappeared. In the final version there remained only the central group with the mother suckling her child, against a solemn landscape, at the same time Norwegian and reminiscent of the trecento style. *History* (Plate 65a) remained the most faithful to the first draft – this rarely successful idea of the Homeric old man in his own native seaside landscape, so classic in its timelessness. Skovgaard in his comment as one of the jurors underlined this very fittingly: 'If the pictures are required to correspond to the Hall and to be Greek in style, then there may be two views on whether these conditions have been fulfilled. They cannot be said to be Greek in style in the architects' sense but they contain a profounder understanding of Greek art, and they are staunchly Greek in conception, so that they would inevitably enhance the Hall (Fig. 7), a circumstance which should earn the architects' gratitude.' Thiis, delivering his verdict, recommended the acceptance of Munch's work in all its essential features and proposed that the completed picture *History* should be acquired and hung or, if preferred, executed afresh in fresco. Here in Vienna we recall that it was Franz Wickhoff who championed Klimt's pictures for the University, unfortunately in vain. As in Vienna, so in

39

Oslo, the wall paintings were rejected by the College of Professors despite the favourable majority of the jury. But in Oslo the battle did not end with this defeat for art. Munch's friends and supporters formed a committee which purchased the picture *History* and had it exhibited in the Assembly Hall after the end of term in 1912. The impression it made and Munch's successes abroad were so great that in 1914 the College's vote swung round in his favour and the paintings remained in their place. The tragedy of Rembrandt's *Julius Civilis* and Klimt's University pictures was not repeated.

Thus was saved a monumental work of timeless, classical validity which sprang, not from an imitation of classical style but from a progressive simplification and intensification of expression. It must nevertheless be borne in mind that the *ultimate* goal which the painter kept before his eyes as he worked, was not attained: the fresco. The original intention had been to execute the work in fresco, an intention expressly stated by Jens Thiis when concluding his verdict. Munch was fully aware of this and formed the character of his canvases accordingly. Tendencies towards the fresco manner are already present in earlier works, particularly in several pictures in the *Frieze of Life. Death in the Sickroom* exists not only in oil but also in casein colours which emphasize surface and line and give the picture the character of a fresco. The same is true of *Melancholia* (1900; Plate 41). While Munch was working on the pictures for the University he painted *Life* (1910; Plate 67), one of his most splendid, freest and yet firmest compositions (once in the proud possession of the Dresden Gallery, now in the Oslo Town Hall). It is a potential fresco. Munch said himself that but for the *Frieze of Life* he might not have been able to carry out the University wall paintings. 'The *Frieze of Life* presents the individual's sorrows and joys, observed close at hand – the university pictures embody the powerful eternal forces.'

The broad surface-treatment, the light tones of the side panels which the sun's rays unite with the central picture so as to form a whole, in defiance of the architectural lines of division, point to the character and technique of the fresco. If the painter, instead of having his time and his strength consumed by contention, had from the outset been left in peace to devote himself to this magnum opus, then this great fulfilment of purpose would certainly have been successful. As it is, even this great work of art is not completely free from tragic time-conditioned frustration.

Munch's enlargement of scope in his old age has a Faustian element, in as much as he turned his interest increasingly towards working people and their daily activities. He voiced his conviction that the future would belong to the workers. They entered his great cycle of life. He followed them in all the varying tasks of their daily life. As early as 1910 in Kragerø he created his magnificently conceived composition the *Snow-Shovellers* (Plate 68), the aspect of which reminds one of the *Bathers* in the triptych. Factory workers and miners followed. In 1916 he portrayed them in an uncannily life-like picture as they hurry home at the end of their shift (Plate 69), rushing towards the beholder as if they intended to walk straight through him. This is a recurrence of the old theme of *Karl-Johan Street*, but this time not as the ghostly vision of a poet obsessed by his day-dreams, but the embodiment of a dynamic rhythm of life common to all humanity, throbbing in the painter's veins as in the heavy labourer's. The same year saw the production of his animated pictures of people at work in the fields: *Man in the Cabbage Field* (Plate 72), *The Women in the Fields* and *The Ploughman*, who, abruptly foreshortened, appears a tiny figure behind the enormous head of his white leader. Munch had already tackled this problem of breath-taking space effects as early as 1912 in the *Galloping Horse* (Plate 73). This violent spatial effect is no longer used to portray panic, terror and agoraphobia as in *The Cry*, but to convey the impression of a horse, its sleigh now empty, galloping away from the snow-covered woodyard. The fact that, with Munch, a feeling of lowering catastrophe surrounds even this snapshot impression, is specific to his art, although the placidity of the driver shows that this is merely an increased tempo in normal working life. The most mature of these representations is the group of *Diggers on the Road* (1920; Fig. 6) going about their work in unison like a powerful machine. There is an unusually functional quality about all these scenes. Munch himself said that Eiffel's and Dutert's steel constructions at the Paris World Fair of 1889 were one of the strongest artistic impressions of his youth. The grand anonymity of the workers united in the rhythm of their toil prompted Munch to plan for the new Oslo Town Hall a monumental painting devoted to the workers and intended as the synthesis of all his other similar scenes. The idea of a cyclic synthesis in order to create a monumental work dominated Munch more than ever in his later years. He built himself gigantic open-air studios in which his huge pictures stood protected from the weather, so that his life's work could be created simultaneously.

The landscape of the earlier decades is pre-eminently a landscape of mood, full of lyrical enchantment, mystical experience, dedication and reverence. The type of landscape that follows the University paintings is an embodiment of the life forces and basic elements of life at work throughout nature. The colours are glowing and intense. The painter's closer spiritual affinity with Van Gogh becomes increasingly clear. The eternal rhythm of the sea is shown, its waves beating against the coast in tireless unison (Plate 70). In a coastal landscape painted in the winter of 1915 (Plate 71) one can breathe the magnificently fresh snowy air and the invigorating salt tang of the sea. The crystal clarity, the life-affirming, masculine strength of the Scandinavian winter is a fitting theme for the mature artist. *The Red House* (1926; Hodin 99) with its intense effects of space provokes a comparison with the flat surface treatment of related pictorial themes of earlier date. Formerly a mighty tree was seen as a *single* large surface, now it is dissected into bundles of sinews, tendons and veins. Space deploys its own dynamics. The forces which create it and give it extension assume visible form, cause planes to advance or recede and lead in a diagonal upward movement to a climax. The geological pressure that forces the earth up into a hill, and the architectural stresses which hold sloping roofs in place over house and shed are fundamentally one and the same thing. Henceforward painting no longer presents the interplay of magically significant lines and surfaces but shows the equilibrium of dynamic forces.

In the beginning, mention was made of the duality in Munch's intellectual world. It would be mistaken to believe that this positive view of life had completely banished from his work the darker side of existence, the daemonic, tragic, and pessimistic elements. This darker side persisted until his dying day, for it is only from its fusion with the radiant, life-affirming, positive aspect of his art that the totality of his work is gained, with all conflicts resolved and thereby vanquished. Here precisely is the most profound justification of the Expressionist artist's mission. The fact that this dualism in Munch's intellectual life did not take the form of Christian religiosity is no doubt attributable to his youthful experiences with a repressive father who bordered on religious mania. He resisted these memories with heart and soul. With Munch the belief in higher powers becomes a tragic belief in fate.

Munch often extolled the radiant beauty of the naked female body. In the painting *Summer* (1915; Oslo, National Gallery) he shows it bathed in light and caressed by the sea breezes on the cliffs of the archipelago. The subject of *Puberty* is taken up again in the splendid painting of about 1917 *Girl seated on the Edge of her Bed* (Plate 75). In the 1920's a dark-haired model inspired him to make a series of nudes which surpass Bonnard and Matisse in the suggestive power of painting. The dazzling white limbs stand out in magnificent contrast to the flowing, raven-black hair and are set off by the glowing colours of an oriental rug on which the model kneels or lies, or which is draped in great folds across a wicker chair beside her (Deknatel 60). But Munch did not stop short at the purely pictorial, like the great French masters.

This great mode of vision is conveyed not merely by the powerful rhythm of his brush-strokes but also by his profoundly spiritual conception, the tragedy of this woman covering herself with her own hair when deprived of all other raiment. Not in vain was one of the pictures entitled: *Despair* (Plate 74) and the other: *Woman in Tears* (Thiis p. 313).

A woodcut of the same period *The Last Hour* (Plate 78) marks the return of all the terror and grief of death-bed scenes, all the catastrophic tension of *Anxiety*. It is a paraphrase of the closing scene of Ibsen's *Pretenders*. The scene is set in the Elgeseter convent. Figures of despair gather in the courtyard: Jarl Skule's family and the three men in armour. Here again in the foreground we have in close-up the pallid disk-like face in which grief has extinguished every feature except the helplessly staring eyes. The barbaric directness of the woodcut technique has lent this scene still greater poignancy of expression than the shifting veils and shadows of lithograph did before.

Munch called one of his latest models, Brigitta, 'the Gothic maiden'. Her tall, erect, slender form, her purely intellectual beauty and noble brow, inspired the spiritualist in Munch with some of his most expressive creations of the 'twenties. We recognize her in the *Bohemian's Wedding*, in printed and painted portraits like the *Young Woman on a Couch* (Plate 76) and in one of his most remarkable woodcuts for Ibsen's *Pretenders*: the *Trial by Fire* (Fig. 5). Her erect figure floats like a bright flame against a dark background and is continued vertically by the arch of a Gothic gateway. In her hands she bears red-hot irons. The rhythm of the gateway is repeated several times in the densely packed crowd with their head-gear shaped like helmets and calottes. This crowd is no more than hinted at by delicate scratches in the wood, but its oppressive reality produces its impact. The crowd surges towards the beholder, at alarmingly close quarters, then it halts, showing one or two gigantic heads staring enthralled at the miracle. Thus, to the very last, Munch's art testifies not only to one who has conquered life but also to one who reveres the miraculous and supernatural, a believer in the spirit.

Munch is, in this century, the artist who has painted the most self-portraits. They become more frequent in his later life, as was the case with Rembrandt. Munch, who always sought in his pictures the effect of unbroken, luminous colour and who shunned a gamut imitating the Old Masters, had the deepest veneration for Rembrandt. These later self-portraits of Munch's venture forth into the same region as Rembrandt's, the region where the intellectual vitality of the creative artist transcends the frontiers of the historical and enters the unchanging world of eternal values. This is possible only to the supreme few,

43

to those endowed with the greatest inner tension, to artists who are also great men. One of the last entries in Munch's journal runs: 'I paint and think in the present; I live in the past and in the future.'

In his early self-portraits Munch often emphasized how close to death was the man overshadowed by fate. He was familiar with death, as he himself showed in one of the late lithographs, and did not quail before it. The creative artist's will to live constantly reasserted itself. 'Without mortal danger and sickness I should have been a ship without a helm,' he said. The Spanish influenza of 1918–19, that angel of death who struck down Klimt in his prime and Schiele in his youth, passed Munch by, but left behind a magnificent memorial in the self-portrait *Spanish Influenza* (Plate 77). The painter, slowly convalescing from his exhausting illness, is shown sitting in a basket chair beside the tumbled sick-bed he has left for the first time, yawning with *taedium vitae* as he contemplates his image in the mirror. In 1926 he painted himself in the dazzling sunshine in the full vigour of autumn standing before the gleaming façade of his house, amidst a luxuriant growth of garden flowers (Langaard, *Selvportretter* 52). Another portrait shows him in the golden light of the already setting sun, palette in hand (Langaard, *Selvportretter* 53), surrounded by fluffy white clouds in the blue sky and by green tree-tops from which rise his studio buildings. But the most moving self-portraits are those of the last years of his life.

The world had become evil and menacing: outside one's doors raged the enemy and lurked the spy. Munch had refused to be harnessed to the triumphal chariot of National Socialism like the friend of his youth, Hamsun. And so the last years of his life were overshadowed and burdened by the cares of existence. The old man oppressed, harried by knavery and stratagems, exclaims with righteous indignation in one of his letters: 'The whole world sees in my art both a spiritual and a cultural value, and I cannot but quote the text: "Man shall not live by bread alone, but by every word that proceedeth out of the mouth of God".' He awakes in the night, all alone, and wanders restlessly through the big, deserted, faintly-lit house *The Wanderer by Night* (1939; Frontispiece). Here we meet this strange 'revenant' suddenly looming up before us, his eyes deep in shadow, leaning forward as if harkening to the night. What sounds does it bring him? Perhaps the deep, swelling chords of the grand piano gleaming in the half-darkness, audible only to the inner ear of his memory, for all sound of music is stilled in this old man's house.

Then there is the other moving self-portrait *Between Clock and Bed* (1940; Plate 79). Outside it is winter; the world lies dead beneath its heavy pall of snow. But in his house the lamps are lit and their golden radiance kindles the colours in the pictures hanging on the wall and sets aglow the bright covers on the bed. It is an artificial festival of sunshine and summer, the warm colours, burning red and citron yellow, vying with a cool night-blue. In the midst of it all he stands, marked with age like a tree soon to be felled, shaky but still standing tall and erect like the panels of the door and the nude figure of the 'Gothic maiden' in the painting on the wall and like the clock which is about to strike the last hour. The light of an Indian summer still glows in the old man's wonderfully visionary, transparent face, but it will fade when the old-fashioned clock strikes the hour of his death. Then his bed, so gay with colour, will receive his body and become that frail craft bound for eternity which he has so often painted. And so Munch stands in that narrow space between clock and bed which is granted to man in his declining years, like a figure of one of those old automatic clock-works on which revolve the Twelve Apostles, the conditions and ages of man, and finally Death who completes the cycle of hours.

In this self-portrait Munch made himself appear more aged and fragile than he ever became. Two self-portraits of 1942 still reveal him as the staunch champion of art that he did in fact remain; one shows him standing idly in front of the sunlit wall of his house, the other is a monumental horizontal picture with a view of the snow-covered garden through the window. This picture diffuses a truly solemn atmosphere: winter in the world outside and winter in himself (Langaard, *Selvportretter* 69), this great old man of the North whose life story reads like a saga. Like a distant echo of the 'Art Nouveau' of long ago, whose ornaments he used to load with such a weight of ideas, the radiator standing near him is transformed into a chain of mysterious, peering, elliptical eyes.

But, like Rembrandt in his old age, Munch also possessed a spirit of reconciliation and an inner sense of humour. This is clear from a self-portrait painted in 1940 which shows the artist at table consuming a cod's head (Plate 80). This old man's face in which are delineated scepticism and understanding, grief and irony, humour and unshakeable faith, has in fact found the sum, the final resultant of all duality and of all contradictions between matter and spirit: the most profound humanity. Munch once made an etching of little Omega kneeling in admiration before a gigantic codfish. This cod has found its way into this picture like a final echo of the daemons of long ago, but now it is reduced to a subservient role like the devil at the feet of the Saints in Gothic cathedrals. The master eats up the daemon who thereby loses his power to frighten, just as the daemon is exorcised by each painting in which he is portrayed.

45

THE PLATES

1. SELF-PORTRAIT. About 1881-2.

2. THE ARTIST'S AUNT (KAREN BJØLSTAD) SEATED IN A ROCKING CHAIR. 1884.

3. THE SICK CHILD. 1885–6.

4. PORTRAIT OF THE ARTIST'S SISTER INGER. 1884.

. PORTRAIT OF THE PHILOSOPHER HANS JAEGER SEATED AT A TABLE. 1889.

6. EVENING HOUR
WITH THE ARTIST'S SISTER
LAURA SEATED IN
THE FOREGROUND. 1888.

7. MILITARY BAND IN
KARL-JOHAN STREET
IN OSLO. 1889.

8. SPRING. 1889.

9. EVENING HOUR WITH THE
ARTIST'S SISTER INGER AND
THE POET BODTKER. 1889.

10. RUE LAFAYETTE. 1891.

II. NIGHT. 1890.

12. PUBERTY. 1894.

13. PORTRAIT OF THE ARTIST'S SISTER INGER. 1892.

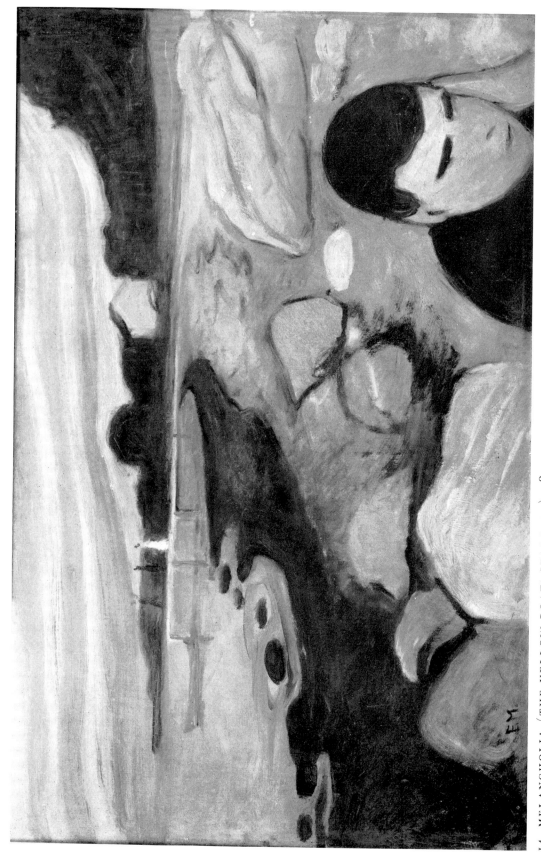

14. MELANCHOLIA (THE YELLOW BOAT; JEALOUSY). 1895.

15. SPRING EVENING IN KARL-JOHAN STREET IN OSLO. 1892.

16. KISS BY
THE WINDOW. 1892.

17. GAMBLING HALL
AT MONTE CARLO
(ROULETTE II). 1892.

18. ANXIETY. 1894.

19. THE CRY. 1893.

20. CHAMBER OF DEATH. About 1894–5.

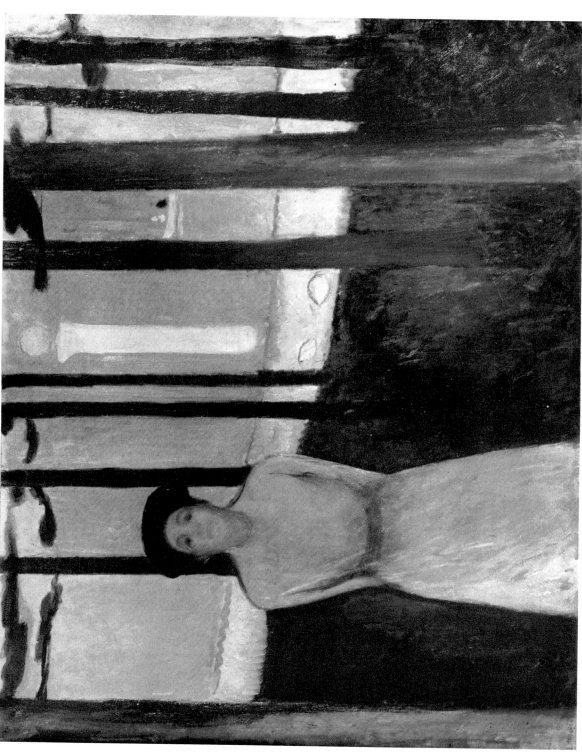

22. THE VOICE. 1893.

24. ASHES. 1894.

25. THE DAY AFTER. 18

26. PORTRAIT OF AUGUST STRINDBERG. 1895.

27. SELF-PORTRAIT WITH CIGARETTE. 1895.

28. THE KISS. Drypoint and Aquatint. 1895.

29. THE KISS. Woodcut. 1897–8.

30. THE PAINTER
PAUL HERRMANN
AND THE PHYSICIAN
PAUL CONTARD. 1897.

32. PORTRAIT OF DAGNY JUELL PRZYBYSZEWSKA. 1893.

33. 'MADONNA'. Lithograph. 1895–1902.

34. THE POET STÉPHANE MALLARMÉ. Lithograph. 1896.

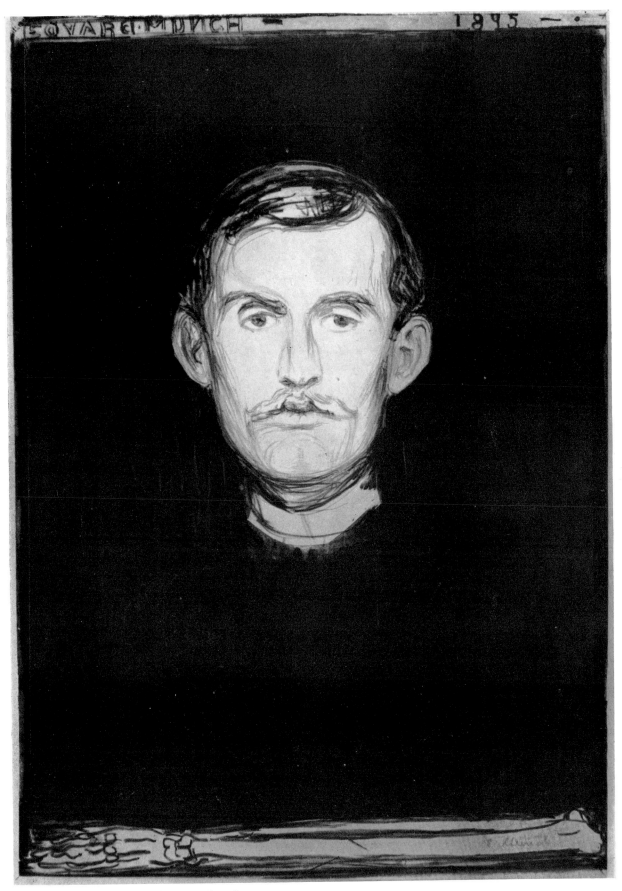

35. SELF-PORTRAIT. Lithograph. 1895.

36. DEATH AGONY.
Lithograph. 1896.

37. THE SICK CHILD.
Lithograph in colour.
1896.

38. THE THREE STAGES OF WOMAN. Lithograph. 1899.

40. HENRIK IBSEN IN THE CAFÉ OF THE GRAND HOTEL AT KRISTIANIA. About 1898.

41. MELANCHOLIA. 1900.

42. VIEW OF OSLO FJORD FROM NORDSTRAND. About 1900.

43. WINTER. 1899.

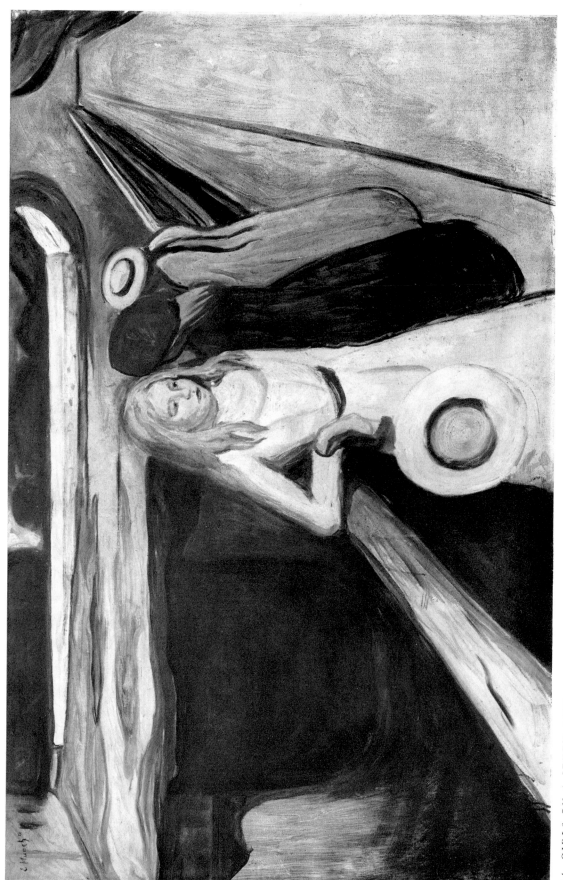

44. GIRLS ON A JETTY. 1900.

45. SUMMER NIGHT
AT THE SHORE. About 1902.

46. GIRLS ON A JETTY. 1901.

47. WHITE NIGHT. 1901.

48. THE DEAD MOTHER. 1899–1900.

49. THE FAMILY ON THE ROAD (GRANDMOTHER, MOTHER AND CHILD). About 1903.

50. 'MADONNA' (LADY WITH THE BROOCH). Portrait of the Violinist Eva Mudocci.
Lithograph. 1903.

51. THE PRIMITIVE MAN. Woodcut. 1905.

52. THE FRENCHMAN: M. ARCHIMARD. 1901

53. THE GERMAN. Portrait of the Cartoonist Herrmann Schlittgen. 1901.

54. SELF-PORTRAIT, WITH BRUSHES IN THE ARTIST'S RIGHT HAND. 190(5).

55. JAPPE NILSSEN. 1908.

56. GROUP OF FOUR GIRLS AT ÅSGÅRDSTRAND. 1902.

57. THE FOUR SONS OF
DR. MAX LINDE. 1903.

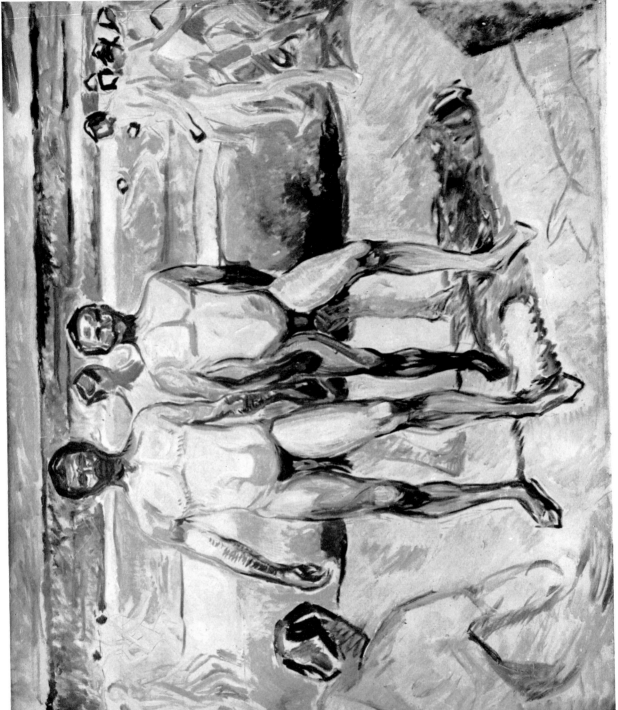

58. MANHOOD. 1907–13.

59. PORT OF LUEBECK WITH A STEAMER. 1907.

60. DR. DANIEL JACOBSEN. 1909(8).

61. SELF-PORTRAIT IN A BLUE SUIT. 1909.

62a. MOUNTAIN OF MEN. About 1925.

62b. THE CRUCIFIED. About 1896.

63. IDEAL PORTRAIT OF FRIEDRICH NIETZSCHE. 1906.

64. THE SUN. 1909—11.

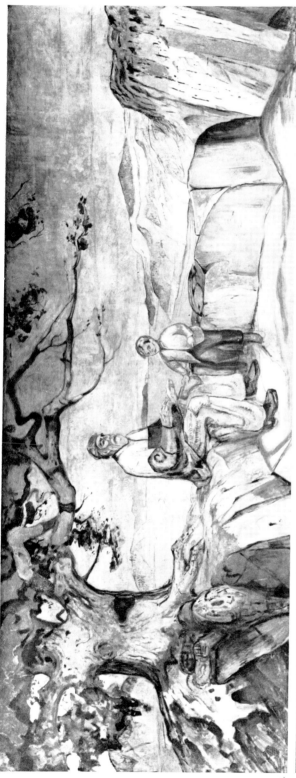

65a

65b

66. ALMA MATER. 1909–11.

69. WORKMEN ON
THEIR WAY HOME. 1916.

70. THE WAVES. 1921.

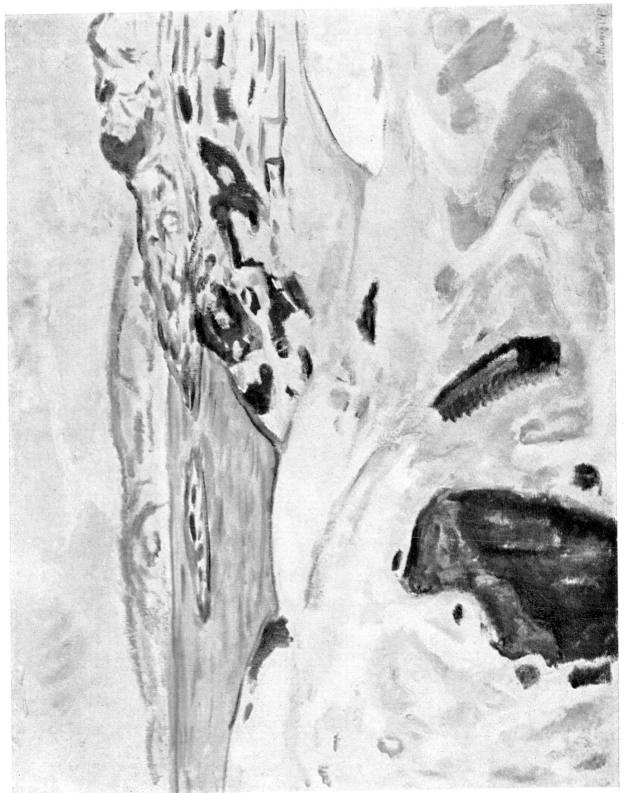

71. COASTAL SCENERY,
WINTER. 1915.

72. MAN IN A CABBAGE FIELD. 1916.

73. GALLOPING HORSE. 1912.

74. DESPAIR. 1919–20.

75. GIRL SEATED ON THE EDGE OF HER BED. About 1917.

76. YOUNG WOMAN SEATED ON A COUCH (BRIGITTE OLSEN). 1925–8.

77. 'SPANISH INFLUENZA'. Self-Portrait. 1ǫ

78. THE LAST HOUR. Woodcut. 1920.

79. 'BETWEEN CLOCK AND BED'. Self-Portrait. 1940.

80. MUNCH EATING A COD'S HEAD. 1940.

NOTES TO THE PLATES

THE ARRANGEMENT of the illustrations tries to follow, in general, the sequence of chronological development. In some cases, however, affinities in content as well as the attempt to offer an aesthetically balanced aspect were decisive for the grouping of the plates.

Munch provided comparatively few of his works with dates. The dating of the undated works is based on exhibition catalogues, on remarks made by the artist to friends and critics, and on recollections of people who witnessed some of the master's works in progress. These sources do not prove reliable in every respect. Even Munch's own memory sometimes went astray, as always happens with great creative artists. The result is a bewildering confusion in the existing literature. A certain clue is given by Schiefler's catalogues of the prints, because this author faithfully followed the artist's graphic work for many years, and his indications may be generally relied upon. But this does not always prove helpful with regard to the paintings. The confusion is increased by the fact that Munch worked on some paintings for years, and by his habit of producing repeated versions of his ideas, the number of which can often only be guessed. The present author was intent upon clarifying the dates of the paintings discussed, but his opinion may be subject to occasional errors. The problem of chronology has been dealt with very seriously by J. H. Langaard in his book *Selvportretter*. The whole situation shows that a complete critical catalogue of Munch's paintings and drawings is urgently needed.

The author wishes to acknowledge with gratitude the help and furtherance which was extended to him by the institutions concerned and by their directors; particular thanks are due to Dr. Harry Fett, Riksantikvar, Oslo and to Mr. Johan H. Langaard, Director of the Oslo Kommunes Kunstsamlinger, who took a lively interest in the publication of this book, also to Mr. Sigurd Willoch, Director of the National Gallery, Oslo; Professor Carl Nordenfalk, Director General of the National Museum, Stockholm; Yngve Berg, Director of the Thielska Gallery, Stockholm; Mr. Ole Rönning Johannesen, Curator of the Bergens Billedgalleri, Rasmus Meyer Collection; Dr. René Wehrli, Director of the Kunsthaus, Zurich; Mr. Harald H. Halvorsen of Oslo, and to two private collectors who kindly provided photographs and permission to reproduce them: Mr. Christian Mustad of Oslo and Mr. Thorvald Johnsen Jr. of Oslo. I should like to extend my thanks also to the Phaidon Press who took every care to have this book published in a dignified form.

Again it is to my wife, Mrs. Eva Benesch, that I am indebted in every possible way for her untiring collaboration in the preparation of this book.

O. B.

NOTES TO THE PLATES

1. SELF-PORTRAIT. About 1881–82. No signature. Oil on canvas. 25 × 18 cm. Oslo, Kommunes Kunstsamlinger. Langaard, *Selvportretter* No. 2.

Painted (in 1881 according to J. Thiis, in 1882 according to J. H. Langaard) in the apartment of Munch's family in Voss-weien. At that time, Munch was attending the drawing school of J. Middelthun and later of W. Holter. In 1882 he began to work as a painter together with his young artist friends in a common studio in the building called 'Pultosten'. The present painting belonged to Munch's sister Inger.

2. THE ARTIST'S AUNT (KAREN BJØL-STAD) SEATED IN A ROCKING-CHAIR. 1884. Signed: E Munch. Oil on canvas. 47 × 41 cm. Oslo, Dr. Harry Fett.

3. THE SICK CHILD. 1885–6. Signed: E Munch. Oil on canvas. 119·5 × 118·5 cm. Oslo, Nasjonalgalleriet.

The composition of this painting occupied Munch for more than four decades. He repeated it in four dated and several undated versions. Compare also the etching of 1894 (Schiefler 7, Willoch 7) and the lithograph No. 37.

4. PORTRAIT OF THE ARTIST'S SISTER INGER (three-quarter length). Signed and dated: E Munch 1884. Oil on canvas. 96·4 × 67·4 cm. Oslo, Nasjonalgalleriet.

5. PORTRAIT OF THE PHILOSOPHER HANS JAEGER SEATED AT A TABLE. Signed and dated: E Munch 1889. Oil on canvas. 108 × 83 cm. Oslo, Nasjonalgalleriet.

Hans Jaeger was also the subject of compositions such as *The Wedding* (Hodin 67) and *The Death of the Bohemian* (Hodin 68).

6. EVENING HOUR WITH THE ARTIST'S SISTER LAURA SEATED IN THE FORE-GROUND. Signed and dated: Edvard Munch 1888. Oil on canvas. 74 × 100 cm. Oslo, Thorvald Johnsen Jr. Collection.

7. MILITARY BAND IN KARL-JOHAN STREET IN OSLO. Signed and dated: E. Munch 1889. Oil on canvas. 102 × 141·5 cm. Zurich, Kunsthaus.

8. SPRING. Signed and dated: E. Munch 1889. Oil on canvas. 169 × 264 cm. Oslo, Nasjonalgalleriet.

See note to No. 3.

9. EVENING HOUR WITH THE ARTIST'S SISTER INGER AND THE POET BØDT-KER. 1889. Signed: E. Munch. Oil on canvas. 150 × 195 cm. Copenhagen, Statens Museum for Kunst.

10. RUE LAFAYETTE. Signed and dated: E. Munch 91. Oil on canvas. 92 × 73 cm. Oslo, Nasjonalgalleriet.

11. NIGHT. 1890. Signed: E Munch. Oil on canvas. 64·5 × 54 cm. Oslo, Nasjonalgalleriet.

The same motif is represented in the etching of 1895, Schiefler 13, Willoch 12.

12. PUBERTY. 1894. Signed: Munch. Oil on canvas. 150 × 110 cm. Oslo, Nasjonalgalleriet.

Replica, painted in Berlin, of the first version of 1886, destroyed by fire. See the note to No. 25. The same subject is also represented in the lithograph, Schiefler 8. The latest version of this subject is the painting in Stockholm, Moderna Galleriet: *Girl seated on the Edge of her Bed*, No. 75.

13. PORTRAIT OF THE ARTIST'S SISTER INGER. Full-length. Signed and dated: E. Munch 1892. Oil on canvas. 172 × 122·5 cm. Oslo, Nasjonalgalleriet.

The solemn figure of Munch's sister frequently appears in representations of the 'Frieze of Life'.

14. MELANCHOLIA (THE YELLOW BOAT; JEALOUSY). 1895. Signed: E.M. Oil on canvas. 65 × 96 cm. Oslo, Christian Mustad Collection.

Repetition of a pastel of 1891. The background scene also appears in the woodcut Schiefler 82 (1896) and in the Frieze at the Freia Chocolate Factory, Oslo, where instead of the solitary man several spectators are to be seen on the shore.

15. SPRING EVENING ON KARL-JOHAN STREET IN OSLO. 1892. Signed: E. Munch. Oil on canvas. 84·5 × 121 cm. Bergen, Billedgalleri. Rasmus Meyer Collection.

16. KISS BY THE WINDOW. Signed and dated: E. Munch 1892. Oil on canvas. 72·3 × 90·7 cm. Oslo, Christian Mustad Collection.

There exists also an upright version of this composition in the Haakon S. Onstad Collection, Munkedal, Sweden. (Glaser, p. 131.) The group of houses in Nice, seen through the window, also forms the subject of other landscape studies of Munch's: *View from a Window with a Cypress*, Harald H. Halvorsen, Oslo (*Exhibition Catalogue*, Vienna 1959, No. 5).

17. GAMBLING - HALL AT MONTE CARLO (ROULETTE II.). Signed and dated: E. Munch 1892. Oil on canvas. 54 × 65 cm. Oslo, Kommunes Kunstsamlinger.

18. ANXIETY. 1894. No signature. Oil on canvas. 93 × 73 cm. Oslo, Kommunes Kunstsamlinger.

The composition is a further development of the idea of *The Cry*, No. 19. The scenic setting is the same. The two strolling figures in the distance have increased to a whole procession of people who move towards the onlooker, like those in *Karl-Johan Street*, (No. 15.) The faces of the more distant ones are like indistinct disks. The three persons in the near foreground recall—hardly by mere accident —the features of Stanislaw Przybyszewski, Munch, and Dagny Juell.

The composition is repeated, with many changes and in reverse, in the lithograph of 1896 (Schiefler 61a, 61b). The latter served as a model for the woodcut version, Schiefler 62. A print of this was inscribed by the artist as follows: 'La nature était comme cloré (colorée) du sang et des hommes passe (passaient) comme des prêtres'.

19. THE CRY. Signed and dated: E Munch 1893. Oil on canvas. 91 × 73·5 cm. Oslo, Nasjonalgalleriet.

A replica is in Oslo, Kommunes Kunstsamlinger. Represented also, in the same direction, in the lithograph Schiefler 32. The setting appears first in a study of Nice, in 1891. In 1892 it was used for the painting *Despair*, Thielska Galleriet, Stockholm.

20. CHAMBER OF DEATH. Signed: E. Munch. About 1894–5. Casein colours on canvas. 150 × 167·5 cm. Oslo, Nasjonalgalleriet. Langaard, *Selvportretter* 5.

Paraphrase of the death of Munch's sister Johanne Sophie who died when Munch was fourteen years old. The members of the family, among them Inger and the artist himself, can be recognized.

The first version of this compositional idea is a pastel in Oslo, Kommunes Kunstsamlinger (*Selvportretter* No. 4). The date inscribed by the artist's own hand on this pastel seems to read 1893. There exists another version painted in

NOTES TO THE PLATES

NOTES TO THE PLATES

oil, 134·5 × 159 cm, Oslo, Kommunes Kunstsamlinger. It resembles the above-mentioned pastel more than the present painting, mainly in the two female figures. The present version is the maturest one, which shows many compositional improvements. It seems to be the third one and served as a model for the lithograph of 1896, in the same direction, Schiefler 73.

21. MOONLIGHT. 1893. Signed: E. Munch. Oil on canvas. 140·5 × 135 cm. Oslo, Nasjonalgalleriet.

The woodcut in colour *Moonlight*, 1896, Schiefler 81, makes use of part of the composition in reverse (the woman is cut short below her shoulders).

22. THE VOICE. Signed and dated: E Munch 1893. Oil on canvas. 88 × 110 cm. Boston, Mass., Museum of Fine Arts.

The painting represents beautifully the mood of the northern summer-night which Munch expressed also in *The Dance of Life* and in different landscapes. The voice of the solitary woman seems to re-echo in the solemn silence of nature. Her figure is lit up by an eery source of light emanating from the lower left corner as if it came from an invisible fire. The mythical power of nature is made visible here as in *The Cry*, No. 19, though not in a frightening way but in an appealing and poetical one. The background setting was repeated by Munch in a landscape painting of 1895 (Oslo, Christian Mustad Collection, Hodin 96). It also forms the scenic setting in the decorative Frieze of the Chocolate Factory Freia in Oslo.

The same subject with slight variations appears in the dry-point *Summer-Night* of 1895, Schiefler 19, Willoch 18.

23. THE STORM. Signed and dated: E. Munch 1893. Oil on canvas. 98 × 127 cm. Oslo, Christian Mustad Collection.

24. ASHES. 1894. Signed: E. Munch. Oil on canvas. 120·5 × 141 cm. From the 'Frieze of Life.' Oslo, Nasjonalgalleriet.

The composition was twice repeated by Munch in lithographs: Schiefler 69 (1896), and 120 (1899). In Schiefler 69 it is transformed into a decorative ensemble; in Schiefler 120 it appears with minor changes in reverse.

25. THE DAY AFTER. 1894. Signed: E. Munch. Oil on canvas. 115 × 152 cm. Oslo, Nasjonalgalleriet.

Replica painted in Berlin. The first version of 1886, painted in Oslo, had been destroyed by fire. Also represented in the etching of 1895 (Schiefler 15, Willoch 14). See the note to No. 12.

26. PORTRAIT OF AUGUST STRINDBERG. 1895 (according to Thiis). Signed: E. Munch. Oil on canvas. 120 × 90 cm. Stockholm, Moderna Museet.

In the following year 1896, Strindberg was portrayed by Munch in the lithograph Schiefler 77.

27. SELF-PORTRAIT WITH CIGARETTE. Signed and dated: E. Munch 1895. Oil on canvas. 110 × 85·5 cm. Oslo, Nasjonalgalleriet. Langaard, *Selvportretter* No. 6.

Related to the transcendent version of the same year which shows the three-quarter-length figure of the artist in the nude, lit up by the flames of hell (Langaard, *Selvportretter* No. 9.)

28. THE KISS. 1895. Dry-point and aquatint. 343 × 278 mm. Schiefler 22b, Willoch 22. Vienna, Albertina.

Two pencil sketches of the figures in Oslo, Kommunes Kunstsamlinger. The etching served as model for a small oil painting on a mahogany panel in the possession of Harald H. Halvorsen, Oslo (Catalogue, p. 12). See also No. 29.

29. THE KISS. 1897–8. Woodcut from two blocks on Japanese paper. 467 × 465 mm. Schiefler 102 B.I. Vienna, Albertina.

Transformation and simplification of the etching No. 28.

30. THE PAINTER PAUL HERRMANN AND THE PHYSICIAN PAUL CONTARD. Signed and dated: E. Munch 97. 54 × 73 cm. Vienna, Kunsthistorisches Museum.

See the note to No. 31.

31. JEALOUSY. Signed and dated EM 9(7). Oil on canvas. 67 × 100 cm. Bergen, Billedgalleri. Rasmus Meyer Collection.

This painting could not have been made before Munch's arrival in Paris in 1896, because he had not met the painter Paul Herrmann—who was the model for the jealous man—earlier than that year. His features are blended with those of Przybyszewski. See Herrmann's own account reported by Erich Büttner, J. Thiis (small edition), p. 91.

A version in lithograph, in reverse, and with considerable changes, also originated in 1896 (Schiefler 58).

32. PORTRAIT OF DAGNY JUELL PRZY-BYSZEWSKA. 1893. Oil on canvas. 149·8 × 112 cm. Oslo, Kommunes Kunst-samlinger.

33. 'MADONNA'. Lithograph in colour, on Japanese paper; the black stone worked in 1895, the three stones in colour in 1902. 557 × 345 mm. Schiefler 33 without the frame. Vienna, Albertina. Based on the painting (in the same direction) of 1894 in the National Gallery, Oslo.

34. THE POET STÉPHANE MALLARMÉ. 1896. Lithograph. Schiefler 79a (without the inscribed name below). About 401 × 289 mm. Oslo, Kommunes Kunstsam-linger.

35. SELF-PORTRAIT. Along the upper border is inscribed: Edvard Munch—1895. Lithograph. 456 × 315 mm. Schiefler 31. Langaard, *Selvportretter* No. 8. Vienna, Albertina.

36. DEATH AGONY. 1896. Lithograph. 393 × 500 mm. Schiefler 72. Vienna, Albertina.

A further development of the painting of the same subject (1895) in Bergen, Billedgalleri, Rasmus Meyer Collection (*Exhibition Catalogue*, Boston 1950, No. 18).

A variant of this composition which enhances its penetrating effect was painted in 1915 and is in the Statens Museum for Kunst, Copenhagen.

37. THE SICK CHILD. 1896. Signed: E. Munch. Lithograph in colour from three stones, on Japanese paper. 421 × 565 mm. Schiefler 59c. Vienna, Albertina.

See No. 3.

38. THE THREE STAGES OF WOMAN (also called THE SPHINX). 1899. Lithograph. 460 × 595 mm. Schiefler 122. Vienna, Albertina.

The composition forms part of the 'Frieze of Life'. Painted version of 1895(?) in Bergen, Billedgalleri, Rasmus Meyer Collection (E. Munch, Utstilling, Bergen 1959, Cat. No. 19).

39. MOTHER AND DAUGHTER. About 1897. No signature. Oil on canvas. 135 × 163 cm. Oslo, Nasjonalgalleriet.

A woodcut in several colours (Schiefler 117) was made by Munch in 1898, as a variant of the idea of the present painting.

40. HENRIK IBSEN IN THE CAFÉ OF THE GRAND HOTEL AT KRISTIANIA. About 1898. Oil on canvas. 70 × 96 cm. Formerly Berlin, Fritz Jonas. Ausstellung E. Munch, Zurich, Kunsthaus 1922,

No. 9. – Ausstellung E. Munch, Berlin, Nationalgalerie 1927, No. 48.

A more stylized version (about 1902) is in Oslo, Kommunes Kunstsamlinger (*Exhibition Catalogue*, Berne 1958, Cat. No. 40).

The present painting is rendered, in the same direction, in the lithograph of 1902, Schiefler 171. Another lithograph (Schiefler 171a) shows a light house to the right of Ibsen's head.

The painting is dated '1898' in the Zurich Exhibition Catalogue and '1895' in the Berlin Exhibition Catalogue. The former date seems more probable, because Munch did not transpose it into the lithograph before 1902.

41. MELANCHOLIA. (Munch's sister Laura has been alleged to be the model, R. Stenersen, p. 91). 1900. No signature. Oil on canvas. 110 × 126 cm. Oslo, Kommunes Kunstsamlinger.

Another version with slight changes and of less arresting force, is in Oslo, Private Collection (*Exhibition Catalogue*, Berne 1958, No. 31). The light of the setting sun casts yellow rectangles on the right wall. Intense red in the table cover. The contrast of the glowing colours conveys the feeling of melancholy, desertion and growing madness. Rendered in the lithograph of 1925–6, reproduced A. Moen, *Age and Milieu*, p. 68 below.

42. VIEW OF OSLO FJORD FROM NORDSTRAND. About 1900. Signed: E. Munch. Oil on canvas. 72·5 × 100 cm. Mannheim, Kunsthalle.

43. WINTER. 1899. Oil on canvas. No signature. 60·5 × 90 cm. Oslo, Nasjonalgalleriet.

44. GIRLS ON A JETTY. 1900. Signed: E. Munch. Oil on canvas. 83 × 128 cm. Zurich, Kunsthaus.

Painted in Åsgårdstrand. It is the first relatively naturalistic treatment of a compositional idea, which Munch varied in quite a number of paintings afterwards. See No. 46.

The same composition appears in reverse in the etching of 1903, Schiefler 200, Willoch 104.

45. SUMMER NIGHT AT THE SHORE. About 1902. Oil on canvas. 103 × 120 cm. Signed: E. Munch. Vienna, Kunsthistorisches Museum (formerly Mrs. Alma Mahler).

The subject matter was treated by Munch first in 1892 'Mystic of a Summer Night', Haakon S. Onstad, Munkedal, Sweden (Hodin, No. 95).

46. GIRLS ON A JETTY. 1901. Signed E M. Oil on canvas. 136 × 126 cm. Oslo, Nasjonalgalleriet.

The same motif as in No. 44 extended by the addition of surrounding scenery. A version in the Wallraf-Richartz Museum (dated 1905), identical in composition, shows the first girl leaning with her back against the parapet as in No. 44.

Two further versions combine the motif with the figure of Aase Nørregaard: one in the Thielska Gallery, Stockholm, showing Aase Nørregaard amidst a group of girls, a group of men being added to the right, another one showing Fru Nørregaard alone in the foreground with a group of ladies on the right (1903). The large tree in the background forms the main subject of a landscape painting of 1904 in the collection of J. B. Stang (Thiis, p. 269). The entire landscape motif of the background in autumnal evening light is rendered in a painting dated 1905 (Oslo, Niels Werring Collection), *Exhibition Catalogue*, Munich 1954–5, No. 61. See also the much later woodcut Schiefler 488 (1920).

47. WHITE NIGHT. 1901. No signature. Oil on canvas. 115 × 110 cm. Oslo, Nasjonalgalleriet.

Variants on the same motif were made by Munch in two horizontal compositions, one in the Kunsthaus Zurich (Munich *Exhibition Catalogue* No. 45, Fig. 34), the other with the smoke of a passing train in Oslo, J. Capellen Collection (*Exhibition Catalogue*, Boston 1950, No. 31).

48. THE DEAD MOTHER. 1899–1900. Signed: E. Munch. Oil on canvas. 100 × 90 cm. Bremen, Kunsthalle.

A variant of this composition is the etching of 1901, Schiefler 140, Willoch 59.

49. THE FAMILY ON THE ROAD (GRANDMOTHER, MOTHER AND CHILD). About 1903. No signature. 197 × 122 cm. Stockholm, Thielska Galleriet.

The date of origin is assumed to be 1903. This is quite plausible if we compare Nos. 56, 57.

50. 'MADONNA'. (LADY WITH THE BROOCH.) Portrait of the Violinist Eva Mudocci. 1903. Lithograph on Japanese paper. 600 × 460 mm. Schiefler 212. Vienna, Albertina.

51. THE PRIMITIVE MAN. 1905. Woodcut. 685 × 458 mm. Schiefler 237. Vienna, Albertina.

The same type of old fisherman appears in the painting 'Two Men in half-lengths'. Oslo, Thomas Olsen Collection (*Exhibition Catalogue*, Berne 1958, No. 86).

52. THE FRENCHMAN (M. ARCHIMARD). 1901. No signature. Oil on canvas. 185 × 70 cm. Oslo, Nasjonalgalleriet.

53. THE GERMAN (PORTRAIT OF THE CARTOONIST HERRMANN SCHLITTGEN). Signed and dated: E. Munch 1901. Oil on canvas. 200 × 120 cm. Oslo, Kommunes Kunstsamlinger.

54. SELF-PORTRAIT WITH BRUSHES IN THE ARTIST'S RIGHT HAND. Full length. Signed and dated: E. Munch

190(5), the figure 5 has been erased. Oil on canvas. 197 × 99 cm. Oslo, Kommunes Kunstsamlinger. Langaard, *Selvportretter* No. 25.

55. JAPPE NILSSEN. Signed and dated: Munch 1908. Oil on canvas. 193 × 93 cm. Oslo, Kommunes Kunstsamlinger.

56. GROUP OF FOUR GIRLS AT ÅSGÅRDSTRAND. 1902. Signed: E. Munch. Oil on canvas. 89·5 × 125·5 cm. Stuttgart, Württembergische Staatsgalerie.

Four versions of the composition exist of which the present one is of the highest quality. Two of them, very similar, are in Oslo, Kommunes Kunstsamlinger. The one in Stockholm, Thielska Galleriet, shows only three girls (dated 1905). The motif occurs also in the Frieze of the Freia Chocolate Factory, Oslo.

57. THE FOUR SONS OF DR. MAX LINDE. Signed and dated: E. Munch 1903. Oil on canvas. 144 × 199·5 cm. Luebeck, Museum.

Munch created also a series of dry-points of the members of the family and of Dr. Max Linde's house: the so-called 'Linde Folio' (Schiefler 176–191). The four sons are shown head-and-shoulders in the dry-point, Schiefler 180.

58. MANHOOD. Centre piece from the Warnemünde Bathers' Triptych. 1907–13. No signature. Oil on canvas. 204 × 230 cm. Oslo, Kommunes Kunstsamlinger.

59. PORT OF LUEBECK WITH A STEAMER. Signed and dated: E. Munch 07. Oil on canvas. 81·5 × 122 cm. Zurich, Kunsthaus.

60. DR. DANIEL JACOBSEN. Signed and dated: Edv. Munch, Kjobenhavn 1909 (8). Oil on canvas. 204 × 112 cm. Oslo, Kommunes Kunstsamlinger.

Munch spent the end of 1908 and the first months of 1909 in Dr. Jacobsen's Sanatorium. The portrait was painted during this period. The last number of the date is probably 9, although it cannot be clearly deciphered.

A small-scale oil sketch is in Copenhagen, Statens Museum for Kunst.

61. SELF-PORTRAIT IN A BLUE SUIT. Painted in the Sanatorium at Copenhagen. Signed and dated: E. Munch Kjøbenhavn 1909. Oil on canvas. 100 × 110 cm. Bergen, Billedgalleri. Rasmus Meyer Collection. Langaard, *Selvportretter* No. 32.

62a. MOUNTAIN OF MEN. About 1925. Oil on canvas. 450 × 780 cm. (dimensions of the original form of the painting without the addition of separate parts of a further treatment of it. Oslo, Kommunes Kunstsamlinger.

The Mountain of Men was originally planned by Munch as the centre piece of the decoration of the University Assembly Hall in Oslo. Although it was discarded and replaced by the picture of the rising sun, Munch continued to work on the idea, probably in the hope of including it in the decoration of the Town Hall in Oslo.

62b. THE CRUCIFIED. About 1896. Oil on canvas. 80 × 120 cm. Oslo, Kommunes Kunstsamlinger.

Illustration to Friedrich Nietzsche's *Thus spake Zarathustra*, Introductory Discourse, Chapter 3: 'The hour in which ye say: What is my pity worth! Is not pity the cross upon which he is nailed that loveth mankind? But my pity is no crucifixion.'

63. IDEAL PORTRAIT OF FRIEDRICH NIETZSCHE. Three-quarter length. Signed and dated: E. Munch 06 Weimar. Oil on canvas. 201 × 160 cm. Stock-

holm, Thielska Galleriet. Harry Fett, *Kunst på Arbeidsplassen. Edvard Munch de unge Ar*. Kunst og Kultur Series, Oslo 1946, p. 26.

Painted in Weimar for the collector Ernest Thiel who, like Munch himself, was an admirer of Nietzsche. The light colours of the painting lend it the character of a large drawing which recalls Toulouse Lautrec's posters.

64. THE SUN. Oil on canvas. 452 × 788 cm. Wall-decoration in the Assembly Hall of the University of Oslo. 1909–11.

65a. HISTORY. Oil on canvas. 452 × 1165 cm. Wall-decoration in the Assembly Hall of the University of Oslo. 1909–11.

See the lithograph of 1914, Schiefler 426.

65b. THE EXPLORERS. Oil on canvas. 452 × 1165 cm. Wall-decoration for the Assembly Hall of the University of Oslo (now replaced by the Alma Mater, see No. 66), 1909–11.

66. ALMA MATER. Oil on canvas. 452 × 1165 cm. Wall-decoration in the Assembly Hall of the University of Oslo. 1909–1911.

This is the final version of the composition first laid out in the *Explorers*. See note to No. 65b, further also the lithograph of 1914, Schiefler 427.

67. LIFE. 1910. Oil on canvas. 196 × 370 cm. Oslo, Town Hall.

Formerly Nationalgalerie, Dresden. The motif of the Tree of Life recurs frequently in Munch's monumental concepts. Compare also the etching, Willoch 177.

68. THE SNOW-SHOVELLERS. 1911. No signature. Oil on canvas. 163 × 200 cm. Oslo, Kommunes Kunstsamlinger.

The idea of the Warnemünde Triptych finds an echo in this composition.

Another version (dated 1910, Glaser, p. 173) gives the composition an upright format. Used also for the projected wall-decoration of the Oslo Town Hall 1935–1944, Stenersen (p. 251). See the woodcut of 1911, Schiefler 350 and the print (lithograph and woodcut combined) of 1912, Schiefler 385.

69. WORKMEN ON THEIR WAY HOME. 1916. Oil on canvas. 202 × 230 cm. Oslo, Kommunes Kunstsamlinger.

Another version is in Copenhagen, Statens Museum for Kunst.

70. THE WAVES. 1921. Signed and dated: E. Munch 21. Oil on canvas. 100 × 120 cm. Oslo, Kommunes Kunstsamlinger.

71. COASTAL SCENERY, WINTER. Signed and dated: E. Munch 1915. Oil on canvas. 103 × 128 cm. Oslo, Nasjonalgalleriet.

72. MAN IN THE CABBAGE FIELD. 1916. Oil on canvas. 136 × 181 cm. Oslo, Nasjonalgalleriet.

73. GALLOPING HORSE. 1912. Signed: E. Munch. Oil on canvas. 148 × 120 cm. Oslo, Kommunes Kunstsamlinger.

See the etching of 1915, Schiefler 431, Willoch 175.

74. DESPAIR. 1919–20. Oil on canvas. Edvard Munch, *Mennesket og Kunstneren* p. 135. Whereabouts and measurements could not be verified.

75. GIRL SEATED ON THE EDGE OF HER BED. About 1917. Signed: E.

Munch. Oil on canvas. 141 × 106 cm. Stockholm, Moderna Museet.

The most mature version of the subject, which first made its appearance in *Puberty*, 1886 (see No. 12).

76. YOUNG WOMAN SEATED ON A COUCH (BRIGITTE OLSEN). 1925–8. Signed: E. Munch 1928. Oil on canvas. 136 × 115 cm. Oslo, Kommunes Kunstsamlinger.

77. 'SPANISH INFLUENZA', SELF-PORTRAIT. Signed and dated: Edv. Munch 1919. Oil on canvas. 150·5 × 131 cm. Oslo, Nasjonalgalleriet. Langaard, *Selvportretter* No. 44.

78. THE LAST HOUR. 1920. Woodcut. 426 × 580 mm. Schiefler 491. Vienna, Albertina.

The woodcut represents the last scene of Act V of Henrik Ibsen's *Pretenders*. The stage setting corresponds exactly to Ibsen's description of the courtyard of Elgeseterkloster. Jarl Skule with Ragnhild, his sister Sigrid, the Abbess, and the three Jarls can be distinguished. The despairing figure in the foreground apparently represents Margaret, Jarl Skule's daughter and King Håkon's wife. See also *Trial by Fire*, Fig. 5.

79. 'BETWEEN CLOCK AND BED', SELF-PORTRAIT. 1940. No signature. Oil on canvas. 171 × 121 cm. Oslo, Kommunes Kunstsamlinger. Langaard, *Selvportretter* No. 67.

80. MUNCH EATING A COD'S HEAD. 1940. Panel. 46 × 34 cm. Oslo, Kommunes Kunstsamlinger. Langaard, *Selvportretter* No. 66.

TEXT ILLUSTRATIONS

Frontispiece: 'THE WANDERER BY NIGHT', SELF-PORTRAIT. 1939. No signature. Oil on canvas. 90 × 68 cm. Oslo, Kommunes Kunstsamlinger. (Langaard, *Selvportretter* No. 65.)

Fig. 1. CHAMBER OF DEATH. 1896. Lithograph. 390 × 555 mm. Schiefler 73. Oslo, Kommunes Kunstsamlinger. See note to No. 20.

Fig. 2. OSVALD'S BREAKDOWN. 1920. Lithograph. About 390 × 500 mm. Schiefler 487. Oslo, Kommunes Kunstsamlinger. Final scene of Ibsen's *Ghosts*.

At the request of Max Reinhardt, Munch made stage designs for Ibsen's tragedy. The same subject is represented, in the same direction, in a painting of 1906, formerly in Berlin, Fritz Hess. – *Ausstellung in der Nationalgalerie*, Berlin 1927, Cat. and Fig. Nos. 108.

Fig. 3. OMEGA AND THE FLOWERS. From the series *Alpha and Omega*. 1908–9. Lithograph. 260 × 187 mm. Schiefler 318. Vienna, Albertina.

Fig. 4. FUNERAL MARCH. 1897. Lithograph. 555 × 370 mm. Schiefler 94. Oslo, Kommunes Kunstsamlinger.

The compositional idea of this lithograph anticipates the *Mountain of Men*. A variant of its visionary content is depicted in the lithograph *In the Kingdom of Crystals*, Schiefler 93, where Munch himself is lying in the coffin raising his head.

Fig. 5. THE TRIAL BY FIRE. About 1927. Woodcut. 460 × 370 mm. Oslo, Kommunes Kunstsamlinger (703).

Brigitte Olsen served as model. The subject is inspired by Inga of Varteig's ordeal of the Branding by Iron in Act I, Scene 1, of Henrik Ibsen's historical play *Pretenders*. Other woodcuts by Munch are also inspired by the same drama: A. Moen, *Age and Milieu*, pp. 66, 67 and Stenersen, (pp. 252 and 255). See also No. 78.

Fig. 6. DIGGERS ON THE ROAD. 1920. Lithograph. About 435 × 610 mm. Schiefler 484. Vienna, Albertina.

A painting, dated 1920, shows the same composition (Thiis, p. 309). Munch planned to insert this group into the left-hand portion of the semi-circular decoration which he prepared for the Oslo Town Hall (Hodin 116).

Fig. 7. INTERIOR OF THE ASSEMBLY HALL OF THE UNIVERSITY OF OSLO with the wall-decorations by Munch. Right: *Alma Mater*. See No. 66.

BIBLIOGRAPHY

BOOKS AND ARTICLES

MULLER, Hannah B., "Edvard Munch. A Bibliography." In: *Oslo Kommunes Kunstsamlinger. Årbok 1946–51*, Oslo 1951.

— — —

DEKNATEL, see Exhibition Catalogues.

FETT, Harry, *Kunst på Arbeidsplassen. Edvard Munch de unge År.* (Kunst og Kultur Series) Oslo 1946, p. 26.

GAUGUIN, Pola, *Edvard Munch*, Oslo 1933, and 1946.

GLASER, Curt, "Edvard Munch als Graphiker." *Kunst und Künstler* 11, Berlin 1913, pp. 570–78.

— — "Edvard Munchs Wandgemälde für die Universität in Kristiania." *Zeitschrift für Bildende Kunst*, N.F. 25, Leipzig 1914, pp. 61–66.

— — *Edvard Munch*, Berlin 1917.

— — "Edvard Munch" in Thieme-Becker's *Künstlerlexikon*, vol. XXV, Leipzig 1931, p. 265ff.

GLØERSEN, Inger Alver, *Den Munch jeg Møtte*, Oslo 1956.

HODIN, J. P., *Edvard Munch*, Stockholm 1948.

JEDLICKA, Gotthard, "Über einige Selbstbildnisse von Edvard Munch." *Wallraf-Richartz-Jahrbuch XX*, Köln 1958, p. 225ff.

KOKOSCHKA, Oskar, *Der Expressionismus Edvard Munchs.* Kleine Gurlitt Reihe No. 12, Wien-Linz-München 1953.

LANGAARD, Johan H., *Edvard Munch, maleren*, Oslo 1932.

— — *Edvard Munchs Selvportretter*, Oslo 1947.

LINDE, Max, *Edvard Munch und die Kunst der Zukunft*, Berlin (1902).

— — *Edvard Munch*, Berlin 1905.

MADSEN, Stephen, TSCHUDI, *An Introduction to Edvard Munch's Wall Paintings in the Oslo University Aula.* 1959.

MOEN, Arve, *Edvard Munch. Age and Milieu*, Oslo 1956.

— — *Edvard Munch. Woman and Eros*, Oslo 1957.

MUNCH, Edvard, *Mennesket og Kunstneren (Reports of his Friends)*, Oslo 1946.

— — *Edvard Munchs Brev. Familien. (Letters)*, Oslo 1949.

NORDENFALK, Carl, *Apropos Munch utställingen*, Stockholm 1947.

PRZYBYSZEWSKI, Stanislaw, *Das Werk von Edvard Munch.* Mit Beiträgen von F. Servaes, W. Pastor, J. Meier-Graefe, Berlin 1894.

SCHIEFLER, Gustav, *Verzeichnis des Graphischen Werks Edvard Munchs bis 1906.* Berlin 1907.

— — *Edvard Munch. Das Graphische Werk 1906–26.* Berlin 1927.

STENERSEN, Rolf, *Edvard Munch*, Oslo 1946. — Stockholm-Frankfurt-Zürich 1950 (German Edition).

SVENAEUS, Gösta, *Idé och Innehål i Edvard Munchs Konst.* Oslo 1953.

THIIS, Jens, *Edvard Munch og Hans Samtid*, Oslo 1933.

— — *Edvard Munch*, Berlin 1934 (Small Edition in German).

TSCHUDI, see MADSEN.

WILLOCH, Sigurd, *Edvard Munch, Etchings*, Oslo 1950.

— — *Edvard Munchs tresnitt (woodcuts).* Catalogue of the Exhibition, Oslo, Nasjonalgalleriet 1946.

Ausstellung Edvard Munch, *Kunsthaus Zürich* 1922 (W. Wartmann).

Ausstellung Edvard Munch in der *Nationalgalerie, Berlin* 1927.

Exhibition *The Institute of Contemporary Art, Boston* (E. Munch by F. B. Deknatel, Introduction by J. H. Langaard). London 1950 (particularly valuable for the Bibliography of Hannah B. Muller, p. 116).

Ausstellung Edvard Munch, *München-Köln* 1954–55.

Ausstellung Edvard Munch, *Kunstmuseum Bern* 1958.

LIST OF COLLECTIONS